Unsung African-American History Makers

Unknown Hidden Figures And Their Stories

Michael A. Carson

Matthew A. Carson

Copyright © 2023 by Michael A. Carson

Double Infinity Publishing
P. O. Box 55 Grayson, GA 30017

Printed in the United States of America

Unsung African-American History Makers

Co-Author: Matthew A. Carson
Research Assistant: Matthew A. Carson
Content Editor: Shenika H. Carson
Cover Design: Double Infinity Publishing
Design Director: Matthew A. Carson

ISBN-979-8-9855087-3-4

Double Infinity Publishing books may be purchased in bulk at a special discount for sales promotion, corporate gifts, fund-raising or educational purposes. For details, contact the Special Sales Department, Double Infinity Publishing, P.O. Box 55 Grayson, GA. 30017 or by email: DoubleInfinityPublishing1@Gmail.com.

DEDICATION

As a Father and Son writing team, my co-author Matthew and I would like to dedicate this book to my beautiful Mother Mary Carson, someone who continues to inspire us, we love you and thank Almighty God for you everyday. You are the Greatest Mother Ever!

Other Publications By Author: Michael A. Carson

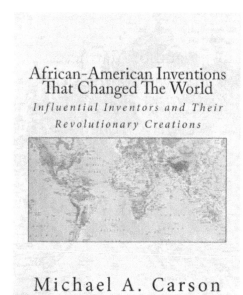

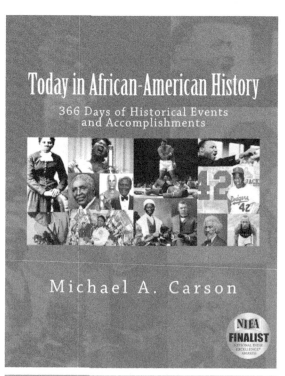

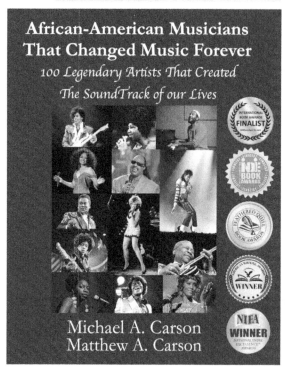

Double Infinity Publishing

Contents

INTRODUCTION

During Black History Month, we pause to salute and reflect on the contributions African-Americans have made to the rich fabric that makes up the United States. There are many untold stories that reveal the best of Americans who stepped up when duty called, broke through barriers, or quietly made their communities better one person at a time.

Not everyone who has helped to change the country and the world always get the credit they deserve, even though their actions are the kind of impact that changes things for the better. There are many hidden figures of untaught history who deserve to be celebrated for their incredible contributions, but their names are left out of the narrative.

Although American history often resonates with the names of many great African-American men and women, there are countless other lesser-known inspiring figures who have contributed significantly and helped to shape American and World history. The African-American story often reflects on struggle, but there are many untold stories of inspiration, innovation, courage, genius and bravery.

Although not widely recognized, the men and women mentioned in this book have made significant contributions to the fields of science, politics, law, technology, civil rights, medicine, and beyond. Their personal stories and experiences may have been often overlooked, but their impact to our society and the world has been monumental. While African-American history is expansive and wide, there are generations of figures and heroes that we may be completely unaware of.

Although scores of little-known individuals helped to shape history, from medical breakthroughs to fighting fearlessly through opposition, this group of historical heavyweights all deserve to be household names, along with their legacies etched into American history. Even though they didn't get the recognition as other historic well known individuals, these hidden figures were just as instrumental. Along with their sacrifices and efforts, their accomplishments were just as pivotal to several historic movements.

Dr. Sadie Tanner Mossell-Alexander

To say that Dr. Sadie Tanner Mossell-Alexander (1898 - 1989) shattered multiple glass ceilings is an understatement, she was the first African-American woman in the United States to receive a Ph.D. in Economics. The Philadelphia native was a leader in legal, political, and civic arenas, and a life-long champion of civil rights and equal opportunity for all, regardless of race or gender. Among her many "firsts," she was the first woman to receive a Law Degree from the University of Pennsylvania Law School, she was also the first African-American woman to practice law in the State of Pennsylvania. She served as secretary for the National Urban League and was later appointed to the President's Committee on Civil Rights by President Harry S. Truman. The committee's report served as the foundation of the civil rights movement in America and was the basis for future civil rights policy decisions and legislation. Mossell-Alexander was the first National President of Delta Sigma Theta Sorority, she was also a founding member of the National Bar Association, an association composed of African-American attorneys, she served as their national secretary. Throughout her career, she was awarded several honorary doctorate degrees, while also having a professorship named in her honor at the University of Pennsylvania, which still continues today.

Economist, attorney, and civil rights activist, Dr. Sadie Tanner Mossell-Alexander was one of the most influential African-American women of the early 20th century. Growing up in Philadelphia, PA., her parents later moved to Washington, D.C. After graduating from M Street High School in in 1915, she was accepted to the University of Pennsylvania. Following her college graduation in 1918, she then entered Graduate School at Penn to study economics. In 1921, she became the first African-American woman in the United States to receive a Ph.D. in Economics.

Mossell-Alexander's accomplishment received media coverage throughout the nation, however, due to racial and gender discrimination, she did not receive any job offers anywhere in the North that would correspond with her economics degree. In 1921, she began working as an Assistant Actuary for North Carolina Mutual Life Insurance Company in Durham, which was the largest African-American-owned insurance company in the United States. In 1923, she left her position in Durham and returned back to Philadelphia to marry Raymond Alexander, who just graduated from Harvard Law School.

Facing continued job discrimination in Philadelphia, she decided to pursue a law degree in the hopes of using the courts and legislation to open doors that were closed to African-Americans throughout the country. In 1924, she enrolled in the University of Pennsylvania Law School. Three years later, she became the first African-American woman graduate of this law school, and the first to pass the Pennsylvania State bar exam. She began working as an attorney at the law firm she established with her husband Raymond named, "Alexander & Alexander." They were both early principal members of the National Bar Association, and their law firm was instrumental in drafting legislation that outlawed racial segregation in Pennsylvania.

As she used her legal expertise to bring civil rights cases to court, President Harry S. Truman took notice, he named her to his Committee on Civil Rights, which he established by executive order. She helped to investigate the status of civil rights in America and proposed measures to strengthen and protect them. As a member if the committee, they submitted a report of its findings to President Truman, this would later become a blueprint for the civil rights movement. Thirty years later, President Jimmy Carter also appointed her as Chair of the White House Conference on Aging, which makes policy recommendations to congress and the president regarding the elderly. As the first National President of Delta Sigma Theta Sorority, Mossell-Alexander also served as secretary of the National Bar Association, becoming the first woman to hold this role in the organization.

Octavius Valentine Catto

Octavius Valentine Catto (1839 - 1871) was a prominent Philadelphia activist, scholar, athlete, and military officer in the National Guard during the civil war. Known as one of the most influential civil rights activists during the 19th century, he fought for the abolishment of slavery and the implementation of civil rights for all. He was prominent in the actions that successfully desegregated Philadelphia's public trolleys and played a major role in the ratification of the 15th Amendment, baring voter discrimination on the basis of race. The civil war increased Catto's activism for abolition and equal rights. He joined with Frederick Douglass and other African-American leaders to form a Recruitment Committee to sign up African-American soldiers to fight for the Union and emancipation. Known as the "19th century Martin Luther King," the city of Philadelphia erected a sculpture to commemorate Catto outside City Hall in 2017, it was the first public monument in Philadelphia to honor a specific African-American figure.

Civil rights activist, scholar, and military officer, Octavius V. Catto was one of the most influential African-American leaders in Philadelphia during the 19th century. Born in Charleston S.C., his family migrated North in the mid-1840's when he was five years old, first to Baltimore, then settling in Philadelphia. Catto was afforded an excellent education, attending Vaux Primary School and then Lombard Grammar School, both segregated institutions.

In 1854, he became a student at the city's Institute for Colored Youth, which later became the nations first Historically Black College and University (HBCU), Cheney University. As he excelled as a student, he graduated valedictorian of his class in 1858. During his early twenties, Catto was one of the most influential African-American leaders in the city of Philadelphia.

The civil war stoked Catto's activism for the abolishment of slavery and equal rights for all men. When the Confederate Army invaded Pennsylvania in 1863, culminating in the Battle of Gettysburg, he responded to the call for emergency troops by raising one of the first volunteer companies, the 5th Brigade of the Pennsylvania National Guard. Serving as Major and Inspector General in the brigade, he was among the first leaders who led the "Call to Arms" recruitment of African-American soldiers.

Catto helped to raise eleven regiments of "Colored Troops" in Pennsylvania. Before being sent to the warfront, the soldiers were organized and trained at "Camp William Penn," which was the first and largest federal training facility for African-American soldiers in the country. He was the highest ranking African-American in the military during the time.

While serving in uniform, Catto founded the Banneker Literary Institute and the Pennsylvania Equal Rights League in 1864, he was also a member of several other civic, literary, patriotic, and political groups. As a civil rights champion, he fought fearlessly for the desegregation of Philadelphia's trolley car system. Known as the "19th century Martin Luther King," he employed civil disobedience tactics as he tirelessly fought for freedom and equality for his community.

After the civil war, Catto started a Philadelphia protest movement that led to the passage of the 1867 Pennsylvania law that prohibited racially segregated public transportation. Later the same year, he and his childhood friend, Jacob White Jr., formed one of the earliest Negro League baseball teams named the "Philadelphia Pythians" of which he was a co-manager and a player. The Pythians were composed of primarily middle class professionals from the surrounding areas of Washington, D.C., Philadelphia, and New York City.

Henrietta Lacks

Some of the most important advancements in modern medical research can ultimately be traced back to an African-American woman who worked on a tobacco farm before World War II, her name is Henrietta Lacks (1920 - 1951). After being diagnosed with cervical cancer at Johns Hopkins Hospital in 1951, a sample of her cells was sent to a tissue lab without her consent. After being examined, it was discovered that Lacks cells did not die, in fact they were doubling at a phenomenal rate as they had the unique ability to replicate every 20-24 hours. Although these weren't the first human cells grown in a lab, this was the first time they survived more than a few days. This huge medical breakthrough allowed researchers to conduct experiments on human cells outside of the body. The cells were given the name "HELA" which is a combination of the first two letters of her first and last name. Although they carry her name, Lacks who passed away at the young age of thirty-one would never know her cells were extracted for scientific research. Despite the ethical debate around the harvesting of Lacks cells, scientist continue to use the immortal HELA cell lines all over the world. They have been linked to thousands of scientific studies on how viruses work and chemotherapy research, they have also played a crucial role in medical cures such as the polio vaccine.

The name Henrietta Lacks may not be well known, but her immense contribution to science, and impact on modern medicine has lasted more than half a century. Growing up in Roanoke, VA., Lacks was a tobacco farmer and mother of five children, but she was also indirectly responsible for one of the biggest medical breakthroughs in history. In February 1951, Lacks went to Johns Hopkins Hospital in Baltimore, MD., the only hospital in the area that treated African-American patients during the time, she was treated for a form of cervical cancer.

While being examined by a doctor, he removed a tissue sample during a biopsy from a tumor that developed in her body to use for his research. He didn't ask for permission or tell her how this genetic sample might be used. The doctor then gave her cells to a Johns Hopkins tissue specialist, who examined them under a microscope and found something he had been trying to find for decades, this discovery was groundbreaking, the findings were soon shared with researchers globally. Most cells typically divide 40 times before dying, but Lacks cells were uniquely different, they continued to duplicate in a control lab environment indefinitely with no signs of slowing down. Although her cells thrived, her health declined and she passed away later that year.

This medical breakthrough was the first so called "immortal" cell line, which is a population of cells with a mutation that allows them to grow and be kept alive indefinitely. Over seventy years later since this discovery, her cells are still replicating, the cells were given the name "HELA" which is a combination of the first two letters of her first and last names. Ever since the original HELA cells from Lacks were put into mass production, they have allowed generations of scientist to perform experiments and critical research in cell biology without having to use an actual living person.

Since the 1950's, researchers have been subjecting her HELA cells to all types of viruses, both to study how the cells reacted, and to develop life-saving vaccines. Since then, hundreds of billions of HELA cells have been created worldwide, which contributed to the development of drugs for numerous ailments, including polio, parkinson disease, and leukemia. Although millions of people worldwide have benefited from HELA cells, and millions of dollars were made through research, there was anger and outrage due to her contribution to science being unknown even to her family until the 1970's, and the ethical debate around retrieving her cells without consent. Her case was an important component in the debate surrounding informed consent from patients for the extraction and use of cells in research. In 2013 the National Institutes of Health (NIH) granted the Lacks family control on how data on the HELA cell would be used going forward.

Robert Smalls

Robert Smalls (1839 - 1915) was a hero of both the civil war and of reconstruction, in 1874, he was elected to the United States House of Representatives from the State of South Carolina. Just twelve years earlier, he staged one of the boldest and most imaginative escapes in the history of slavery, his courage and timing were unbelievable. Smalls was enslaved until the age of twenty-three as he was pressed into service for the Confederacy aboard a ship called The Planter. For nearly a year, he became skilled at working on the ship, he quietly observed the movements of the ship and its crew as he eventually advanced to the position of pilot. He knew that the Confederate crew trusted him. He had his eye on freedom, all he needed was an opportunity. Just before dawn on May 13, 1862, he took his chance. While the ship's officers slept ashore, Smalls and his fellow enslaved crew members pulled up anchor and eased The Planter into Charleston Harbor. The plan of the crew was to meet up with their family members, then take off and sail towards Union territory. He knew there would be danger ahead because they needed to pass through four Confederate checkpoints. Smalls impersonated the captain giving hand signals as he passed each checkpoint. As dawn broke, he slipped past all four checkpoints undetected. As the ship approached Union territory, he replaced the rebel flag with a white surrender flag narrowly avoiding cannon fire. Smalls, along with the entire crew were finally free.

Mastermind, war hero, and politician, Robert Smalls was born in Beaufort, S.C., in 1839. Growing up as an enslaved child, he was permitted to work in nearby Charleston by the age of twelve as a laborer. In his later teen years, his love of the sea lead him to find work on Charleston's docks, as a result of varies experiences, he became very knowledgeable about Charleston harbor. At the age of eighteen, he met Hannah Jones, an enslaved hotel worker. Smalls sought permission to marry and live with her in an apartment in Charleston.

He became skilled at working on ships, eventually advancing to the position of pilot. In 1861, he was hired to work on a steamer called "The Planter," which was used to transport cotton to ships headed to Europe. Once the civil war began, Confederates seized the ship in order to use it as an armed transport vessel. Having won the confidence of the commander, he was a trusted crew member. Smalls and his wife always had an eye on freedom, all they needed was an opportunity, soon after they began to plot their escape.

Smalls and seven other enslaved crewmen carried out his escape plan on May 13, 1862. In the evening, the officers all left the ship, Smalls and the crew took the ship, met their families at a pre-arranged location in the harbor and fled to the Union blockade. They were able to successfully pass through all Confederate checkpoints as Smalls impersonated the captain giving hand signals he observed from the true captain of the ship. His escape plan succeeded, as his family and crew were free. He later proved to be a valuable resource for Union forces, as he had extensive knowledge of Charleston's Harbor and military configurations.

He quickly became known throughout the North as a hero, newspapers and magazines began reporting the story about his ingenious escape, shortly after, he visited Washington D.C. Smalls was instrumental in persuading President Abraham Lincoln to permit African-Americans to fight for the Union. Recruited as a valuable member of the Union Army, he later became a Captain, making him the first African-American to command a United States war ship.

Following the civil war, the South went through a period of reconstruction, and the 15th Amendment granted African-Americans the right to vote. After serving in the military, Smalls went into business and politics. In 1874, he was elected to the United States House of Representatives, where he served two terms representing South Carolina's 5th Congressional District. His district was mostly African-American voters, who all exercised their constitutional right to vote for the first time during the election.

Frederick Douglass Patterson

Frederick Douglass Patterson (1871 - 1932) was the first African-American to own and operate a Car Manufacturing Business. Greenfield-Patterson cars were built in Greenfield, OH. Beginning in 1865, the company originally known as C.R. Patterson and Sons, built fashionable carriages. Patterson inherited the company from his father in 1910 and began building motorized vehicles. The first Patterson automobile rolled off the line on September 23, 1915. The company produced approximately 150 vehicles. Considered to be a better quality vehicle than Henry Ford's "Model T," the company's two models were the Roadster and a four-door Touring, both cars were sold for the price of $850. The Patterson-Greenfield car had a forty horsepower, four-cylinder engine and reached a top speed of fifty miles per hour. While the Ohio company created a beautiful, well-made vehicle, it couldn't compete against Detroit's flourishing industry giants on efficiency or price. If the company was to survive, it would need a new venture, one that would prove more successful than automobile manufacturing. Patterson then turned to producing custom bodies for commercial vehicles, his son Frederick Jr. handled the design work, making him the third-generation Patterson in the family business. The company would continue to use the Patterson-Greenfield name up until 1921, when they reorganized as the Greenfield Bus Body Company.

Entrepreneur, known for running the family business, Frederick Douglass Patterson was the first African-American to build motorized cars. Named after the abolitionist, Frederick Douglass, Patterson grew up in Greenfield, OH. In 1865, his father, Charles Patterson founded the company C. R. Patterson and Sons, which specialized in building fashionable horse carriages. In 1888, Frederick attended Ohio State University where he played football, he became the first African-American to ever play for the team. In his senior year, he left the university and taught school in Louisville, KY., for two years.

Patterson inherited and took over the company upon the his father passing away in 1910. After he assumed leadership of the business, he noticed the rise of "horseless carriages," and he began development of the first Patterson-Greenfield automobile, which completed in 1915. The Patterson-Greenfield sold for $850, it had a reputation of being a higher quality automobile than Henry Ford's "Model T." Unfortunately for Patterson, the Model T had cornered the automobile market, it initially sold for $825 in 1908 when first introduced to the public, but over the years as Ford production expanded, the price by 1915 was $360, the year the first Patterson-Greenfield debuted.

Despite the quality of their vehicles, the business faced problems of scale. In an era of rapid development of the use of assembly lines and integration of the manufacturing business (both led by Ford), there was no way for Patterson to produce a medium-priced car effectively. From 1915 to 1920, the company produced 150 Patterson vehicles of two styles, the two-door roadster and the big four-door touring car. C.R. Patterson and Sons could not obtain capital to continue manufacturing the automobiles. The company was forced to cease vehicle production and returned to a focus on vehicle-repair services.

During the 1920's, competition from Detroit became increasingly more intense. Patterson recognized the need to diversify and modernize. He reorganized his fathers business under the name Greenfield Bus Body Company and capitalized on high regional demand for school bus and truck bodies constructed on Dodge, Chevrolet, Ford, and International chassis. In 1929, nearly half of the school buses in Ohio were made by Patterson. This new focus allowed Greenfield to remain profitable through the decade and for its products to reach a broader regional market and beyond. The Great Depression had a devastating effect on the company, as widespread financial problems caused customers to cut back on bus orders. In 1939, after seventy-four years of providing fine transportation, the company that had made carriages, automobiles, and buses closed its doors.

Mary Ellen Pleasant

Mary Ellen Pleasant (1815 - 1904) was perhaps the most powerful African-American woman in the Gold Rush Era of San Francisco during the 1850's. As an abolitionist, she earned her title as the "Mother of California's early civil rights movement." She worked on the underground railroad across many states and then helped bring it to California during the Gold Rush Era. Pleasant established several restaurants for California miners, she made a fortune through her various businesses and became one of the richest and most powerful people in the state of California. Pleasant was a real estate innovator and millionaire, she also helped to establish the Bank of California. Despite her considerable wealth, she worked as a housekeeper for some of San Francisco's most prominent wealthy citizens. These jobs provided her with free investment advice that she gathered from conversations between rich and powerful people. She was a prolific investor in the real estate and mining boom industries in the mid-19th century.

Abolitionist, entrepreneur, and civil rights activist, Mary Ellen Pleasant may not be a household name, but her story rivals any great American entrepreneur. Born in Philadelphia, PA., in 1815, Pleasant was sent by her parents at a young age to work for a Quaker family in Massachusetts as a clerk at the family store, slavery had essentially been illegal in the state since the end of the 18th Century. While working at the shop she learned to read and write, but she never had a formal education. Her family was deeply involved in the abolitionist movement. She later met her first husband, James Smith, a carpenter and contractor. When he passed away, he left her a large inheritance, which she used to continue her abolitionist work.

Pleasant worked as a conductor on the underground railroad across many states for several years, she assisted hundreds of enslaved people to find their freedom from the South through various routes into Canada. Due to her reputation for helping so many, she soon became a hunted slave rescuer while in New Orleans, which forced a move to California. She moved to San Francisco in 1852 during the Gold Rush Era.

She began working as a domestic servant and chef for wealthy families. These jobs provided her with free investment advice as she secretly increased her own wealth based upon conversations that she overheard from many local tycoons as she attended to them during meals and conferences. Pleasant used the knowledge she gained to open several restaurants, a string of laundries and boarding houses, she was also a co-founder of the Bank of California. Pleasant built a massive investment portfolio that was reportedly worth as much as $30 million, a fortune that would make her close to a billionaire in today's value.

Her second husband John Pleasant worked with her for more than two decades as an abolitionist, together they secretly financed and brought the underground railroad to California, finding homes and employment for African-Americans who travelled west, earning her title the "Mother of California's early Civil Rights Movement." In San Francisco, she built a 30 room mansion that spanned two city blocks, the building served as a meeting place for men and women involve in the civil rights movement. During her lifetime, there were hundreds of newspaper articles written about her due to her being a savvy businesswoman and activist. During the reconstruction era, she helped to end racial discrimination on California streetcars by suing a San Francisco streetcar company for continuing to deny service to African-Americans. The North Beach and Mission Railroad Company was forced to pay Pleasant $500 in damages, this decision by a lower court was upheld by the California State Supreme Court in 1868.

Bass Reeves

Bass Reeves (1838 - 1910) was the first African-American Federal Law Enforcement Officer on the early Western Frontier of the United States. For thirty-two years he was a U.S. Deputy Marshal and one of the greatest frontier heroes in U.S. history. During the civil war, Reeves moved to a Native-American territory where he lived among the Cherokee, Creeks and Seminoles. He stayed with these tribes and learned their languages until he was freed by the 13th Amendment, which abolished slavery. Native-American territory was notoriously lawless, and many outlaws fled there to escape justice. In 1875, President Ulysses S. Grant appointed a new judge of the U.S. Court for the Western District with the goal of addressing lawlessness in the territory. Having heard of Reeves knowledge of the territory and his familiarity with the people, he was appointed and worked in the new federal territory which later became Oklahoma and Arkansas. Known as the real "Lone Ranger," he shot and killed 14 outlaws in self-defense during his career and was credited with arresting more than 3,000 felons. He was the most feared and respected lawman of the territory. Along with having a long and distinguished career, he is credited as one of the first American heroes who bridged the gap between the Wild West and the modern world.

Law enforcement official, historically noted as the first African-American U.S. Deputy Marshal west of the Mississippi, Bass Reeves was one of the greatest lawmen in history. Born enslaved in Arkansas, Reeves grew up in Grayson county, TX. In 1861, he escaped and ran North to the area of modern Oklahoma that was then known as Native-American territory, a vast area covering several thousand square miles, it was home to five native tribes. The law worked differently within its boundaries and there was zero state authority for thousands of miles.

Reeves became incredibly familiar with the territory, he learned to speak all of the local tribes languages, he also improved his shooting and tracking skills and felt at home in the Wild West. When President Abraham Lincoln signed the Emancipation Proclamation of 1863, all enslaved people were legally free. Reeves then left the Native-American territory and headed to Arkansas to run a small farm. Following the civil war, he worked as a guide for U.S. government officials interested in traveling through Native-American territory. The land had become a safe haven for outlaws and criminals, Reeves was able to make substantial money as a scout and tracker for federal officers.

His knowledge of native territories and fluency in local languages was brought to the attention of the U.S. Marshals, the agency had been tasked of clearing the area of wanted outlaws. In 1875 he was commissioned to be a Deputy U.S. Marshal by federal judge Isaac Parker of the Western District of Arkansas. While carrying out law enforcement duties for the government, he began arresting and bringing in wanted criminals, Reeves would often travel in a small group along with a Native-American tracker to assist him. Well known for his courage, he killed 14 outlaws and apprehended more than 3,000 throughout his tenure, he was involved in numerous shootouts but was never wounded.

Reeves life story was the inspiration for the fictional character "Lone Ranger." Although fictional "Western" Hollywood motion pictures were rarely accurate in representing life on the Western frontier, an estimated 30-35 percent of cowboys in the late 1800's were African-American. The Lone Ranger was one of the most popular characters of the "Wild West." In the early 1950's, the television show became a worldwide phenomenon. Known as the real Lone Ranger, Reeves did not wear a mask, but he was known to often used disguises when capturing outlaws. In 1907, he retired from federal service and began working as a city police officer in Muskogee, OK. While serving for two years in downtown Muskogee, it was reported there was never a crime committed on his beat.

Cathay Williams

Cathay Williams (1844 - 1893) is the first African-American woman to enlist and serve in the United States Army. Nearly eighty years before women were officially allowed to serve in the army, Williams did so after she passed the initial medical examination. Though this exam should have outed her as a woman, the army did not require a full medical exam during the time. In 1866, she disguised her gender and pretended to be a man in order to enlist. She enlisted under the name "William Cathay" and served as one of the earliest recruits in Company A of the 38th Infantry, a newly formed African-American U.S. Army Regiment. Standing 5'9", Williams was taller than her fellow privates and garnered no curiosity or suspicion. As one of the tallest privates in her company, she amazingly concealed her femininity and fought in the war for over two years despite numerous army hospital visits. While serving in New Mexico she contracted smallpox and was hospitalized, this caused strain on her body along with the desert heat and years of marching. Due to her frequent hospitalizations, the post surgeon finally discovered she was a woman and informed the commander. Williams was then honorably discharged in 1868. Though her discharge meant the end of her tenure with the army, she signed up with a new emerging all-African-American regiment, she then became the only known female to serve with the Buffalo Soldiers.

Soldier and unforgotten hero, Cathay Williams is viewed as a pioneer to all women who served in the United States Armed Forces. Born enslaved in 1844, Williams grew up in Jefferson City, MO. During her adolescence, Union forces occupied Jefferson City in the early stages of the civil war in 1861. She supported the Union Army as a camp follower, at which she traveled with the troops, working as a cook and laundress.

She began supporting the Union Army at the age of seventeen, by the time the war ended, she was twenty-two, and the army was all she had known as an adult. Along with the civil war being over and enslaved people across the country being free, she enlisted in the army. She disguised her true gender posing as a man under the name "William Cathay" and was sent to the 38th U.S. Infantry Regiment.

The unit was organized in 1866 as one of six segregated African-American infantry regiments, which later became collectively known as the "Buffalo Soldiers." The 38th's primary mission was protecting the construction of the intercontinental railroads, the first of which was completed in 1869, when the 38th merged with the 41st Infantry Regiment. The 41st was also a segregated unit, which had spent time in Louisiana and Texas.

As one of the tallest privates in her company, Williams concealed her femininity for two years despite numerous army hospital visits. Incredibly, five hospital visits during her soldier days never revealed her secret. The only thing that kept her from completing her enlistment was when she contracted the smallpox virus. After recovering, she rejoined the 38th, which was then in New Mexico.

After suffering years of stress on her body, frequent hospitalizations and never fully recovering from her smallpox infection, her true gender was finally discovered by the Fort Bayard post surgeon. She was honorably discharged in 1868 on a surgeon's certificate of disability and moved to Fort Union, New Mexico. In fact, her discharge, after nearly two years of service, never mentioned her womanhood. Her commanding officer cited the reason she was unable to continue her military service was due to a disability.

Williams was the only documented African-American woman who served in the army in the 19th century, she set the precedence against all odds. Historically she prevailed, despite the illness, hardship, and discrimination she faced during her life. Along with her service, she carved a small but symbolically important place in the history of American women, African-Americans, and the U.S. Army.

Oscar Micheaux

As one of the most prolific African-American independent filmmakers in the history of American cinema, Oscar Micheaux (1884 - 1951) was a quintessential self-made man. Having the desire to control the production and distribution of his films was the hallmark of his career. In 1917, he self published a book that altered his future forever titled, "The Homesteader," which he later adopted into a silent film in 1919. This motion picture began his career as the first major independent producer-director of African-American films. He wrote, produced, and directed over 40 feature-length films between 1919 and 1948. After World War I, Micheaux persuaded the best African-American actors during the time to star in his films, which appealed to the rapidly growing African-American urban audiences who were happy to see themselves represented on the silver screen. His work critiqued the stereotypes of African-Americans typically depicted in Hollywood films during the time. Audiences were now introduced to a new range of characters on screen who were assertive, articulate, and sophisticated. The actors in Micheaux's films played the roles of doctors, businessman, detectives, and lawyers. His movies provided a window into African-American life and their perspective on race. His work sought to entertain, while also delivering social commentary, he covered issues that were not being covered in films during the time. His work has also been preserved by the Library of Congress and the National Film Registry as "culturally, historically, and aesthetically significant."

Author, director and independent producer, Oscar Micheaux is considered the most influential African-American filmmaker of all time. Growing up in Metropolis, IL., he later moved to Chicago at the age of seventeen. He began working as a Pullman porter on the railroads, which was considered prestigious employment for African-Americans, as it was relatively stable, paid well, and enabled travel across the country. Working as a porter was an informal education for Micheaux, as he made contacts, gained knowledge about the world through traveling, and earned a greater understanding for business.

In 1904, he moved to South Dakota and became a successful homesteader. The government's Homestead Act allowed citizens to acquire a free plot of land to farm. Micheaux began writing about his experiences on the frontier. In 1913, he published his first novel "The Conquest: The Story of a Negro Pioneer," which was loosely based on his own life as a homesteader. The novel attracted attention from a film production company in Los Angeles, which offered to adapt the book into a motion picture. Negotiations fell apart when Michaeux wanted to be directly involved in the film's production, he then decided to produce the film himself.

After setting up his own film and book publishing company, Michaeux released the motion picture, "The Homesteader" in 1919. The film launched his career, and gained praise from critics, one of them calling it a "historic breakthrough," as well as a "credible, dignified achievement." In 1920, he followed up his successful production with a second motion picture titled, "Within Our Gates," which directly challenged the heavy-handed racist stereotypes shown in D.W. Griffith's film "The Birth of a Nation."

Micheaux was the first African-American to have his motion pictures shown in Caucasian-owned movie theaters. He used his films to portray racial injustice suffered by African-Americans, covering topics such as lynchings, mob violence, and discrimination. Given the restrictions of the time, the message in his films were nothing short of groundbreaking.

Over the course of his prolific career, he wrote, produced, and directed over 40 feature-length films. Eventually Hollywood recognized both Micheaux's genius and his crucial role in opening opportunities for African-Americans in front of and behind the motion picture camera. In 1987, he was memorialized on the Hollywood Walk of Fame and posthumously awarded several times by the Black Filmmakers Hall of Fame.

Claudette Colvin

Before civil rights icon, Rosa Parks refused to give up her seat on a segregated bus in Montgomery, AL., in 1955, there was a brave fifteen year old girl who also chose not to give up her seat and move to the back of a crowded Montgomery bus nine months earlier, that young girl name was Claudette Colvin (1939 -). After her refusal to give up her seat, Colvin was arrested on several charges, including violating the city's segregation laws. The National Association for the Advancement of Colored People (NAACP) briefly considered using Colvin's case to challenge the segregation laws in Alabama, but they decided against it due to her young age. She also had become pregnant and they thought an unwed mother would attract negative attention in a public legal battle. Local leaders felt Rosa Parks would be a better figure for a test case for integration because she was an adult, had a job, and had a middle-class appearance, they also felt she had the maturity to handle being at the center of potential controversy. While her role in the fight to end segregation in Montgomery may not be widely recognized, Colvin helped advance civil rights efforts in the city. She was also a member of the NAACP Youth Council, where she formed a close relationship with Rosa Parks, who later became her close friend and mentor.

Civil rights activist and crusader, Claudette Colvin was the first woman to be detained for her resistance on a Montgomery AL., city bus, however, her story isn't nearly as well-known as Rosa Parks. As a child growing up in segregated Montgomery in the 1940's, Colvin witnessed many injustices and unfair treatment of African-Americans in her community. As a teenager, she began learning more about influential African-American historical figures in school during black history month. As a fifteen year old student with aspirations of becoming a civil rights attorney, she attended Booker T. Washington High School.

While returning home from school on March 2, 1955 on a segregated city bus, she was confronted by the bus driver who ordered her to give up her seat to a Caucasian passenger. As Colvin recalled, "It felt like Sojourner Truth was on one side pushing me down, and Harriet Tubman was on the other side of me pushing down, I couldn't get up." She refused to comply with the bus driver's order, saying she paid her fare and it was her constitutional right to remain seated. Shortly after, two police officers arrived and arrested her. The incident occurred nine months before Rosa Parks would be charged with the same crime in the same city.

Colvin and the three other young women who were harassed on that bus in 1955, became the plaintiffs in a lawsuit challenging city bus segregation in Montgomery as unconstitutional. Browder vs. Gayle went all the way to the Supreme Court, where the justices found that Montgomery's bus segregation was in violation of the 14th Amendment, which was a significant civil rights victory. As Colvin and the three other young women fought to challenge Alabama's segregation laws in court, local NAACP organizers believed that as an adult woman, Parks would be a more sympathetic public figure for the national attention the movement soon garnered, but Colvin paved the way.

Along with Colvin and Parks acts of defiance, the Montgomery bus boycott soon became an important symbol of the modern civil rights movement. It was ultimately Colvin's court case victory that outlawed segregation on public transportation in Alabama and ended the thirteen month long Montgomery bus boycott that began after Rosa Parks was arrested. During the time, Colvin was unfazed when Parks became the face of the bus boycott, she was pleased that adults in her community had followed in her footsteps and took a direct stand in the face of discrimination, but retrospection later lead her to a different feeling. Colvin's story of refusing to give up her seat went untold for several decades, after retiring as a nurse in New York City, she then claimed her place in history as a pivotal player in the struggle for racial equality during the civil rights era.

Dr. Charles Richard Drew

Anyone who has ever had a blood transfusion owes a great debt to
Dr. Charles Richard Drew, (1904 - 1950) his immense contributions to
the medical field made him one of the most important scientists of the 20th
century. Drew helped to develop America's first large-scale blood banking
program in the 1940's, earning him accolades as "The Father of the Blood
Bank." During the time, racial segregation limited the options for medical
training for African-Americans, leading Drew to attend medical school
at McGill University in Montréal, Canada. He then became the first
African-American student to earn a Medical Doctorate from Columbia
University, where his interest in the science of blood transfusions led
to groundbreaking work separating plasma from blood. This made it
possible to store blood for a week, which was a huge breakthrough for
doctors treating wounded soldiers in World War II. In 1940, Drew led an
effort to transport desperately needed blood and plasma to Great Britain,
then under attack by Germany. The program saved countless lives and
became a model for a Red Cross pilot program to mass-produce dried
plasma. Drew also pioneered the "blood mobile," which was a refrigerated
truck that collected, stored and transported blood donations to where they
were needed, this vehicle is standard today as it is frequently used by
the Red Cross to collect blood. Drew's contribution to modern medicine
is monumental, he educated and motivated generations of physicians
worldwide.

Surgeon and medical researcher, Dr. Charles Drew was one of the most important scientists of the 20th century, due to his pioneering research and systematic developments in the use and preservation of blood plasma. Growing up in Washington D.C., Drew won a sports scholarship for football and track and field at Amherst College in Massachusetts in 1922, where a biology professor piqued his interest in medicine.

Like many other fields during the 1920's, medicine was largely segregated, greatly limiting education and career options for African-Americans. The narrowed road lead Drew to attend medical school at McGill University in Montréal, Canada in 1926. While earning his Doctorate at Columbia University in the late 1930's, he conducted research into the properties and preservation of blood plasma.

He soon developed efficient ways to process and store large quantities of blood plasma in "blood banks." Due to his expertise in collecting, processing and storing blood, it led to an appointment to head the Blood for Britain Project (BFB), an effort to transport desperately needed blood and plasma to Great Britain, which was under attack by Germany. As the world leading authority in the field, he organized and directed the blood-plasma programs of the United States and Great Britain in the early years of World War II. In 1941, he was named Medical Director of the American Red Cross National Blood Donor Service, his work sealed his reputation as a pioneer and earned him the title, "Father of the Blood Bank."

He recruited and organized the collection of thousands of pints of blood donations for American troops. It was the first mass blood collection program of its kind. The Red Cross excluded African-Americans from donating blood, making Drew himself ineligible to participate in the very program he established. That policy was later modified to accept donations from African-Americans, however the institution segregated blood from African-American and Caucasian donors, throughout the war Drew was outraged by this policy and openly criticized it as "unscientific and insulting to all African-Americans."

Soon after, he resigned from the Red Cross and began working at Howard University, serving as Head of the Department of Surgery and Chief of Surgery at Freedmen's Hospital. His mission was to "train young African-American surgeons and place them in strategic positions, he fought to break down racial barriers for African-American physicians nationwide. He believed this would be his "greatest and most lasting contribution to medicine."

Robert Abbott

As the founder of one of the most read African-American owned newspapers in the United States, Robert Abbott (1870 - 1949) gave voice to an African-American point of view that had been rendered mute in the early 20th century. Abbott graduated from Hampton University, after college he moved to Chicago, IL., where he earned a Law Degree from Kent College of Law in 1898. After experiencing difficulty finding employment as a lawyer due to his race, he then turned to journalism. Armed with a printing background and academic credentials, he converted a 25¢ investment into the Chicago Defender Newspaper. The Defender became the literary domain for racial advancement, it actively promoted the Northern migration of African-American Southerners, particularly to Chicago. The columns not only reported on the movement, but also contributed to a massive movement of African-Americans from the South to cities in the North, Abbott coined the term "Great Northern Drive." By the early 1920's, The Defender's circulation reached more than 200,000 readers per week. Distribution of the paper was facilitated by African-American railroad porters who both sold and distributed the newspaper. The Defender mentioned injustices, but also had a spirit that represented unapologetic African-American pride, dignity, and assertiveness.

Civil rights advocate, attorney, and newspaper publisher, Robert Abbott is known as the first African-American media mogul in the United States. Born just five years after the civil war ended, he grew up in St. Simons Island, Georgia. Abbott was profoundly impacted by his parents, throughout his childhood he was heavily influenced by education and equality. As a young man, Abbott studied the printing trade at Hampton University, he then earned a Law Degree from Kent College in Chicago in 1898.

For several years, he attempted to earn a living as a lawyer, he experienced difficulty finding employment due to his race in Gary, IN., and then Topeka, KS. Abbott found it difficult to support himself as a lawyer. He became convinced that he could defend his people in public print better than he could in a courtroom, he then relocated to Illinois and turned to journalism. In 1905, he founded the Chicago Defender weekly newspaper.

He initially sold hundreds of copies of the four-page paper by going door-to-door, visiting every barbershop, pool room, drugstore, and church on the South Side of Chicago. He then wanted to take his publication national, his main distribution network was made up of African-American railroad porters, who were highly respected among the African-American community, they began selling and distributing his newspapers on trains that travelled all across the country.

By 1916, The Defender's circulation reached 50,000 readers per week, two years later, it climbed to 125,000 readers, and achieved an unprecedented 200,000 per week by 1920. The Defender was arguably the nation's most important African-American newspaper. The paper attacked racial injustices, particularly lynchings in the South. Abbott not only encouraged people to migrate North for a better life, but to fight for their rights once they got there, he described the North as a place of prosperity and justice.

The Defender considerably influenced the Great Migration, the period when large numbers of African-Americans moved from the South to urban areas in the North following World War I, it became the most widely circulated African-American newspaper in the country. Known as "America's Black Newspaper," its success resulted in Abbott becoming one of the first self-made African-American millionaires of the 20th century.

The newspaper's success made Abbott an important figure locally and nationally. The Illinois governor named Abbott to the Chicago Commission on Race Relations, The Defender also contributed broadly to the development of a national African-American culture. Abbott's House in Chicago, and childhood home in Georgia were both designated National Historic Landmarks in 1976.

Maggie Lena Walker

At the turn of the 20th century, Maggie Lena Walker (1864 - 1934) was one of the most influential business leaders in the United Sates. She gained national prominence in 1903 when she founded the St. Luke Penny Savings Bank. Walker served as the Bank's First President, which earned her the recognition of being the first African-American woman to charter a bank in the United States. Later she agreed to serve as Chairman of the Board of Directors when the bank merged with two other Richmond banks to become "The Consolidated Bank and Trust Company," the bank thrived as the oldest continually African-American-operated bank in the United States. Walker's entrepreneurial skills transformed African-American business practices while also inspiring other women to enter the field. As an advocate of African-American women's rights, she also served on the board of trustees for several women's groups. Among them were the National Association of Colored Women (NACW) and the Virginia Industrial School for Girls. To assist with race relations in her community, she helped to organize and served locally as Vice President of the National Association for the Advancement of Colored People (NAACP) and was a member of the National NAACP Board. As a leader and businesswoman, her success and vision offered many economic opportunities to African-Americans and women across the country.

Entrepreneur and teacher, Maggie Lena Walker achieved national prominence as a businesswoman and community leader. Born Maggie Lena Draper, she rose from a modest childhood as a daughter of an enslaved woman in Richmond, VA. As a youth, Walker helped her mother who worked as a laundress, but was also a gifted student. In secondary school, she worked part time as a clerk, first with the "True Reformers," then with the "Independent Order of St. Luke" (IOSL). After graduation, Walker became a teacher and maintained involvement in the IOSL.

The IOSL was organized and lead by African-American women, it played a significant role in African-American community development in the late 19th and early 20th centuries. The organization was dedicated to social reform and service work, they also offered life insurance to the African-American community, later becoming one of the most successful insurance agencies in the nation. In 1886, Walker married Armstead Walker Jr., a brick contractor. Walker had to quit her job, because Virginia laws did not allow married women to teach.

Walker chose to use her position among the African-American elite to influence activism and engage in business enterprises, she pursued business opportunities as a co-owner of the all female, women's union that operated a grocery store, boarding house, and school. To advance her business skills, she enrolled in night school taking accounting classes. She assumed leadership of the IOSL in 1899 and remained in that position until 1934. She encouraged members to be resilient and vigilant in the face of Jim Crow era discrimination and marginalization, under her leadership the IOSL grew to over 100,000 members in 22 states. The IOSL was also the largest employer of African-American women in Richmond.

In 1902, Walker established the ST. Luke Herald, an African-American newspaper in Richmond, she used the earnings from the newspapers financial success to establish the St. Luke Penny Savings Bank in 1903. St. Luke provided loans to the community, by 1920 the bank helped Richmond residents purchase over 600 homes. As President of the bank, she became the most prominent and powerful woman in the banking industry throughout the country.

Walker was often the only woman present at banking conventions, she used her position to advocate for female excellence and representation in the financial world. During the great depression, St. Luke merged with two other banks in the Richmond area to become The Consolidated Bank and Trust Company in 1909, which later became the longest African-American controlled bank in U.S. history.

Richard Allen

Minister, Richard Allen (1760 - 1831) was a pioneer, hero, and trailblazer. Born enslaved, he became a Methodist preacher, outspoken advocate for racial equality, and founder of the African Methodist Church (AME), one of the largest independent African-American denominations in the country. In July, 1794, he converted the interior of an old blacksmith shop and founded Bethel AME Church in Philadelphia. The church became enormously successful, by 1810, membership rose from the original 40 members to over 400. The church grew into Philadelphia's most important institution for African-Americans. Along with Allen's leadership, other African-American Methodist churches began forming in New York, New Jersey, Delaware and Maryland. On April 9, 1816, Allen and other African-American Methodist preachers hosted a meeting in Philadelphia to bring these churches together to form a new denomination, the "African Methodist Episcopal Church" (AME). Allen was elected Bishop, making him the first African-American Bishop in the United States. As an abolitionist, he also maintained his home as a stop on the underground railroad. Allen's vision has echoed throughout history as he influenced several iconic activists including Frederick Douglass and Dr. Martin Luther King Jr.

Minister, educator, and writer, Richard Allen was one of the most influential African-American leaders of the 18th century. Born enslaved in 1760 in Philadelphia, his family was relocated to Delaware when he was eight years old. Allen was allowed to attend a local church, there he attended classes weekly where he learned how to read and write. He converted to Methodism at the age of seventeen after hearing a traveling Methodist Minister preach, as he strongly protested and spoke out against slavery. After attaining his freedom at the age of twenty, he took the last name "Allen" and returned to Philadelphia.

Allen then joined St. George's Methodist Episcopal Church, where African-Americans and Caucasians often worshiped together. Occasionally he was asked to preach to the congregation, as an assistant minister he conducted prayer meetings for African-Americans. He grew frustrated with the limitations the church placed on him and other African-American parishioners, which included segregated pews. Allen left the church as part of a mass walkout with the intention of creating an independent Methodist church.

Allen recognized that African-Americans needed a place they could worship in freedom, he wanted to establish an independent congregation. In 1794, he purchased an old frame building (formerly a blacksmith shop) and created the Bethel (AME) African Methodist Episcopal Church, which was located in Philadelphia. This would be the first African-American church or meeting place that was erected in the United States, a denomination quickly came together over the next few months.

African-American ministers from across the mid-Atlantic region gathered in Philadelphia along with their congregations joined in a fellowship with Bethel AME. Allen was ordained an Elder, then as a Bishop, making him the first African-American to hold such an office in America. Following Allen's example, many African-American Methodists began forming African Methodist Churches in Northeastern cities. Because all experienced similar challenges of being segregated in their previous congregations, Allen organized a convention of African-American Methodists in 1816 to address their shared problems.

Allen oversaw the rapid growth of the AME's mother church in Philadelphia, which grew to seven-thousand members in the 1820's. The denomination became by all accounts the most significant African-American institution in the 19th century. Since its inception, AME has grown to over six-thousand churches and over two-million members worldwide.

6888th Central Postal Directory Battalion

The 6888th Central Postal Directory Battalion was a unique U.S. Army unit and it had the distinction of being the only all-African-American, all-women unit deployed overseas during World War II. The women kept mail flowing to nearly seven-million soldiers in the European Theater of Operations (ETO). The Women's Army Corps (WAC) of the U.S. Army was created by a law signed by President Franklin D. Roosevelt on July 1, 1943. The WAC was converted from the Women's Army Auxiliary Corps which had been created in 1942 but did not have official military status. New WAC recruits underwent four to six weeks of basic training, which included a physical training program, often followed by four to twelve weeks of specialist training. First Lady Eleanor Roosevelt and civil rights leader Dr. Mary McLeod Bethune successfully advocated for the admittance of African-American women as enlisted personnel and officers in the WAC. The 6888 performed their job honorably, the example they set opened the doors for generations of servicewomen. In 2021, the U.S. Senate passed legislation to grant Congressional Gold Medals to the Battalion.

By February 1945, America had been at war for four long years. Military personnel, civilians and the Red Cross were all sent overseas, far away from their families and friends, the only form of communication back home was their mail deliveries. Millions of soldiers began experiencing their letters not arriving due to a backlog of undelivered mail. The U.S. Army understood the importance of mail and decided to send in a special unit to fix the morale busting problem. Warehouses in Birmingham, England began to fill up with over twenty-million pieces of undelivered mail and Christmas packages intended for members of the U.S. military and civilians serving in the European Theater of Operations (ETO).

There was a significant shortage of soldiers who were able to manage the postal service for the Army overseas. Civil rights activist, Dr. Mary McLeod Bethune worked to get support of the First Lady, Eleanor Roosevelt, for a role for African-American women in the war overseas. African-American owned newspapers also challenged the Army to have meaningful jobs for women of color as well.

Army officials reported that the lack of reliable mail delivery was hurting morale amongst the troops, one general predicted the backlog in Birmingham would take six months to process. A group of young African-American women who wanted to serve during the war while crossing racial barriers were up to the challenge. Led by Major Charity Adams, the 6888th Central Postal Directory Battalion, nicknamed the "Six Triple Eight," was an all-African-American battalion of the Women's Army Corps (WAC). Arriving in Birmingham, the 855 women of the Six Triple Eight were met with unheated warehouses stacked to the ceiling with unopened packages and letters.

Despite poor working conditions, these devoted servicewomen worked 7 days a week, 24 hours a day in three eight hour shifts. They achieved unprecedented success and efficiency in solving the military's postal problems, they broke all Army records for sorting mail. Along with the new tracking system Major Adams and the Six Triple Eight Battalion created, the women processed 65,000 pieces of mail per shift and cleared the six month backlog of Birmingham mail in just three months. This unit provided essential support for the military in the European theater by linking service members to their loved ones back home.

With their mission in England complete, the 6888 transferred to France in June, 1945, where they faced a similar stockpile, once again it was cleared in half the time expected. By the time they completed their mission and left France in 1946, they exceeded all expectations. Due to their success, it opened many doors for other African-American women in the Army and other military services.

31

Gladys West

Over the span of a lifetime, the world has changed in ways that would have been virtually unimaginable in the first half of the 20th century. From smart phones, the internet, modern electronics to computers, everyday life is vastly different from a century ago. One technology that has been revolutionary for our society and the world is Global Positioning System (GPS), which was developed by mathematician Gladys West (1930 -). Her scientific contributions has enabled us to understand the shape of the earth well enough to make GPS technology possible. In 1956, West was hired to work at the Naval Surface Warfare Center in Dahlgren, VA., which is operated by the U.S. Navy. When she started her job, the Navy was bringing in new computers. Her duties were programming and coding for the huge machines. She specialized in large-scale computer systems and data-processing systems for the analysis of information obtained from satellites. She was the very first person to put together models of earth's shape to significant precision to enable the existence of GPS in the 1970's. She literally wrote the guide for teaching others how to provide calculations for an accurate survey of earth. Her groundbreaking work played a pivotal role in creating the technology. The U.S. Department of Defense (USDOD) originally put the satellites into orbit for military use, but they were made available for civilian use in the 1980's.

Mathematician and trailblazer, Gladys West is known for her contributions to the mathematical modeling of the shape of the earth. Her innovation and genius pioneered the way for the highly valued technology of Global Positioning System (GPS). Born in a rural county South of Richmond, VA., her parents owned a small farm in an area populated mostly by sharecroppers. She realized at an early age that she did not want to continue farming as an adult, she decided education would offer another path.

As the valedictorian of her high school graduating class, West received a full scholarship to Historically Black College and University (HBCU) Virginia State University, where she earned a Degree in Mathematics in 1952. She later returned for a Master's Degree and graduated in 1955. In 1956 she was hired as a mathematician by the U.S. Naval Proving Ground, a weapons laboratory in Dahlgren, VA. West was admired for her ability to solve complex mathematical equations by hand. She eventually transitioned from solving those equations herself to programming computers to do it for her.

One of her first major projects was work on the Naval Ordinance Research Calculator (NORC), an award-winning program designed to determine the movements of Pluto in relation to Neptune. Admired by her colleagues for her skill in calculating complex mathematical equations, she excelled in programming computers. She then became project manager for "Seasat," an experimental surveillance satellite designed to provide remote sensing of the earth's oceans, it was the first project to demonstrate that satellites could be used to observe useful oceanographic data.

West began analyzing data from satellites, she then programmed a computer to deliver increasingly precise calculations of the Earths surface. By teaching a computer to account for gravity, tides, and other forces that act on earth's surface, West and her team created a program that gave precise calculations. These calculations made it possible to determine a model for the exact shape of earth, her data ultimately became the basis for GPS. She then rose through the ranks and worked on satellite measurements that made GPS more accurate.

Due to her findings, anywhere in the world, signals can be transmitted by a network of earth orbit satellites, pinpointing a position. Similar to the now famous NASA mathematicians Katherine Johnson, Dorothy Vaughan, and Mary Jackson, West is often called one of history's "hidden figures." During the 20th century, many individuals, often African-American women, insightful contributions to science went unrecognized during their time, largely due to their race or gender.

33

Jack Johnson

In 1908, Texan, Jack Johnson (1878 - 1946) defeated Canadian, Tommy Burns to become the first African-American World Heavyweight Boxing Champion. Admired for his quick footwork and defensive style, he was known as the "Galveston Giant," as he defended his heavyweight title from 1908 until 1915. His success in the ring made him an international celebrity during the early 20th century and he was celebrated with several parades in many African-American communities. Outspoken, confident, and conspicuous with his wealth, Johnson intentionally provoked many naysayers who despised his success. During his reign, promoters actively sought out a "Great White Hope" to defeat him as he was an impactful, self assured champion, his victories were often marred by racial discord. Most upsetting to the press and public opinion was his open challenge to society's disapproval of interracial dating and marriage, which was illegal in many states. Three of his marriages were to Caucasian women. Likely in retaliation for his brazenness, he was arrested for violation of the "Mann Act," transporting a woman across state lines for an "immoral purpose." He was found guilty in 1913, even though the woman in question was his wife. After the verdict he fled to Europe, eventually returning to the United States to serve a one-year prison sentence in 1920. As an admired champion, Johnson was also a prolific inventor, he received a U.S. Patent for his invention of the modern day wrench in 1922.

Heavyweight Boxing Champion, Jack Johnson is widely regarded as one of the most influential boxers of all time. Born, in Galveston, TX., to formally enslaved parents, his childhood took place after reconstruction and during the beginning of segregation in America. He attended five years of school, like all of his siblings, he was expected to work at a young age to help support his family. By the age of sixteen, he was on his own, traveling to New York and later Boston before returning to his hometown.

By the early 1900's, the 6'2" Johnson, who had become known as the "Galveston Giant" made a name for himself in the boxing circuit, and had his eyes set on the world heavyweight title. Many Caucasian boxers refused to fight him, as they would not fight or spar with their African-American counterparts during the time. Johnson's talents and reputation were too hard to ignore. Finally, on December 26, 1908, the outspoken and confident Johnson, who often taunted his opponents as he beat them soundly, got his chance for the title when champion Tommy Burns fought him in Sydney, Australia.

The fight lasted until the 14th round before being stopped by the police in front of over 20,000 spectators, Johnson was declared the winner, becoming the first African-American Heavyweight Champion of the World. His skill as a championship fighter, along with the wealth it brought made it impossible for him to be ignored, his victories were often marred by racial discord as promoters actively sought out a "Great White Hope" to defeat him in the ring.

He was flamboyant, regularly dated Caucasian women, and often flaunted his wealth. In a time when African-Americans enjoyed few civil rights and liberties, his success and defiant behavior were a serious threat to the status quo of the Jim Crow era. As the reigning champion for over seven years, he strongly believed African-Americans were not inferior to any other race. Johnson's success frequently made him a target outside of the ring, in 1913, he was put under federal indictment and charged with the "Mann Act."

After being convicted, he escaped and fled to Europe, for the next seven years he lived in exile as he continued to box and defend his title. He returned home to the United States in 1920 and surrendered to federal agents, one year later, he was released in 1921. Johnson continued fighting professionally until the age of sixty. During his boxing career, he fought 93 fights, winning 80 matches, 45 by knockouts. Muhammad Ali often spoke of how he was heavily influenced by Johnson. Although he experienced a life of adversity and a constant battle of prejudice, he never surrendered his pride, and was a man that lived without fear.

Catherine Street Copeland

During the early 1960's, Catherine Street Copeland (1941 -) shattered several glass ceilings in New York City, as she was the first African-American woman to work at NYU Hospital as a Phlebotomy Technician as well as the first Clinical Laboratory Technologist at the New York Blood Center. As a trailblazer in both fields, her expertise and leadership was largely responsible for the success of her departments. As a Phlebotomist Technician, Copeland helped pioneer the profession for women of color in the city as her place in New York history dates back to years of service at Coney Island Hospital, Bellevue Hospital, and Downstate Medical Center. Her role as a Clinical Laboratory Technologist was two-fold, as she worked in the blood bank as well as the operating room, she was an essential part of the medical community. Being on the front line of the healthcare industry, her research was cutting-edge as to what was being done at the time to preserve blood and make higher quality blood products for transfusions into patients. Copeland personally saved a life of a patient who lived abroad by donating her own blood that was shipped to the Country of Iceland, her blood type matched a patient in desperate need. She was equally a profound source of inspiration for her colleagues, she lived her life through faith and was a strong believer in God, she often conducted prayer groups with staff and patients. As a pioneering woman who helped to change the course of healthcare and race relations in New York, Copeland paved the way for future generations of Lab Technologists.

Renown researcher, educator, and crusader, Catherine Street Copeland was a pioneer in the medical field in New York City during the early 1960's. As a prominent member of the medical community, her contributions were recognized by many. Growing up in Brooklyn, N.Y., as the second-youngest of nine children, she received spiritual inspiration and guidance from her mother Mabel Street at an early age. After displaying a passion for healthcare, she was encouraged to study in the medical field after graduating from Clara Barton High School. She then attended City College of New York, and Mandel Technical College.

Eager to encourage greater equality for African-American women, she pursued a career in Phlebotomy and applied to NYU Hospital as a technician in 1961. She believed patient education was paramount, she interacted with the public by conducting interviews while screening for potential donors. Copeland was not only the first African-American in the department, she helped pioneer the profession with her expertise and leadership. She then went on to earn her license to become a certified Clinical Laboratory Technologist for the State of New York. Copeland became the first African-American to work in the Blood Bank for the New York Blood Center (formally the American Red Cross).

Laboratory Technologists are vital to the medical community, as they supervise the collection, separation, delivery, and storage of blood components. Copeland held several roles, including being an instructor who trained students about blood storage, she also worked closely with operating room (OR) technicians to assist with open heart surgeries and transfusions. She taught extensively about blood typing, crossmatching, and how each unit is broken down into components such as blood cells, plasma, and platelets. She advanced the understanding that one unit of blood could be transfused to several patients, each with different needs.

As an amazing figure who was recognized throughout New York City for her contributions, she was also well known as a spiritual comforter to patients and staff. Along with providing their healthcare needs, she offered spiritual and emotional support as well. Living her life through faith, she recognized Almighty God is a divine healer. She organized and oversaw prayer groups as well as provided resources to give comfort to patients, families, and colleagues.

Throughout her forty-three year career, Copeland continued to serve the citizens of New York City. She continued to pioneer the profession for women of color by engaging in quality improvements for patient care and organizational policies. Being recognized as an expert, she mentored many others to help prepare them for leadership positions before retiring and relocating with family to Clayton, N.C.

Asa Philip Randolph

Asa Philip Randolph (1889 - 1979) was a labor organizer and one of the most influential political strategists of the 20th century. His belief in organized labor's ability to counter workforce discrimination and his skill in planning non-violent protests helped gain employment advancements for African-Americans throughout the country. In 1925, he founded the Brotherhood of Sleeping Car Porters (BSCP). He secured membership in the American Federation of Labor for the BSCP, making it the first African-American labor union in the United States. Building upon his efforts with organized labor, Randolph developed non-violent strategies to protest discrimination in the Defense Industries and the U.S. Armed Forces. In 1941, they planned to march in Washington, D.C. to protest discrimination in the Defense Industry. The proposed march pressured President Franklin D. Roosevelt to issue an Executive Order abolishing discrimination in the Defense Industry. In 1947, Randolph planned another march in Washington, D.C. to protest segregation in the military. Once again, the proposed march placed political pressure on the government, and in 1948 President Harry S. Truman issued an Executive Order ending segregation in the military. Randolph's call for civil disobedience to end segregation in the U.S. Armed Forces helped convince the next generation of civil rights activists that non-violent protests and mass demonstrations were the best way to mobilize public pressure. He was often referred to as the true "Father of The Civil Rights Movement."

Labor unionist and civil rights activist, A. Philip Randolph was an influential figure in the struggle for justice and equality for African-Americans. Born in Crescent City, FL., he spent his early years in Jacksonville. He later attended Cookman Institute and graduated as valedictorian in 1907. After graduation, Randolph was inspired by the writings of W.E.B. Du Bois book "The Souls of Black Folk." He was convinced that the fight for social equality was more important than almost anything else, he relocated to New York City in 1911, and settled in Harlem.

In 1917, Randolph founded and became co-editor of a new magazine for African-American readers named, "The Messenger." In 1925, he then established the nations first predominantly African-American labor union called the "Brotherhood of Sleeping Car Porters," which improve working conditions for the nearly 10,000 African-American railroad employees. The Brotherhood would enjoy longstanding prominence in the labor and civil rights movements.

Randolph became the most widely known spokesperson for African-American working-class interests in the country. In 1940, with President Franklin D. Roosevelt refusing to issue an executive order banning discrimination against African-American workers in the Defense Industry, Randolph called for 10,000 African-American citizens to march in Washington, D.C. Support grew so quickly that soon he was calling for 100,000 marchers to converge on the capital.

Pressed to take action, President Roosevelt issued an executive order, which was six days before the march was to occur, declaring "There shall be no discrimination in the employment of workers in Defense Industries or government because of race, creed, color, or national origin." Roosevelt also set up the Fair Employment Practices Commission to oversee the order. After the passage of the Selective Service Act of 1947, Randolph demanded the government integrate the U.S. Armed Forces. He founded the League for Non-Violent Civil Disobedience Against Military Segregation and urged young active members to refuse to cooperate with Jim Crow laws while serving.

Threatened with widespread civil disobedience and needing the African-American vote in his 1948 re-election campaign, President Harry Truman ordered an end to military discrimination in 1948. During the 1950's, Randolph taught other civil rights leaders how to utilize non-violent protests to oppose racial discrimination. Along with Dr. Martin Luther King, Jr., Randolph was one of the principal organizers of the 1963 March on Washington, which brought over 200,000 people to protest segregation. He was also among the leaders that met with President John F. Kennedy after the march.

Lusia "Lucy" Harris

Lusia "Lucy" Harris (1955 - 2022) is considered to be one of the pioneers of women's basketball, she reigned supreme as the "Queen of Basketball" in the 1970's, dominating the game and inspiring a generation of athletes. During her college years at Delta State University, the 6'3" Mississippi native was the center of attention as she helped her team win three straight National Championships from her sophomore through her senior year. In 1976, women's basketball became an Olympic sport for the first time. As Harris played for the USA team, she was the first woman to score a basket in the Olympics. Harris was one of the most influential athletes of the 20th century, as she is the first and only woman ever drafted by the National Basketball Association (NBA). In 1977, she was drafted by the New Orleans Jazz who expressed great interest in her ability. She was unable to participate in the Jazz training camp due to being pregnant at the time. Even though she was unable to play for the Jazz due to personal reasons, she still managed to get selected in the draft ahead of 33 other male players. Although Harris never played in the NBA, her legacy is unmatched, her jersey is retired at Delta State University and she is the first African-American woman inducted into the Naismith Memorial Basketball Hall of Fame and the Women's Basketball Hall of Fame.

Professional basketball player, Lusia "Lucy" Harris was one of the most dominant players in woman's basketball history. Growing up in Minter City, MS., Harris and her siblings attended Amanda Elzy High School in Greenwood, MS., where she played basketball. She won the most valuable player award three consecutive years from 1971 to 1973, and served as Team Captain, she also made the state all-star team and led her school to the state tournament in Jackson, MS. After graduating from high school in 1973, Harris attended Delta State University.

During her freshman year there, she helped the Delta State Women's Basketball team to a 16-2 record. She then led her team to three consecutive Women's basketball NCAA Division III National Championships. She then graduated from Delta State University with a Bachelor's Degree in Health, Physical Education, and Recreation in 1977. She also played on the United States Women's Basketball teams where they won gold medal in the 1975 Pan American Games and silver medal in the 1976 Summer Olympic Games in Montreal, Canada.

On June 10, 1977, Harris made history, the NBA held its annual draft at Madison Square Garden, where she once dropped 47 points in a game during her college days. In the seventh round with the 137th overall pick, the New Orleans Jazz (now Utah Jazz) selected Harris, making her the first and only woman ever officially drafted, there were 33 male players drafted after her selection.

The NBA did not veto the Jazz selection of Harris, and she became the first and only woman to ever be drafted by an NBA franchise. Despite her remarkable basketball skillset and having the opportunity to compete on a professional team, she never played a game in the NBA. She declined to try out for the Jazz because she was pregnant at the time and was unable to participate in the team's training camp.

Harris only experience at the professional level later came as a member of the Houston Angels in the Women's Professional Basketball League for the 1979-80 season. After her playing days ended, she worked as an Assistant Basketball Coach at Delta State University, and in 1984 she received her Master's Degree in Education from her alma mater. She then became the Head Coach of Texas Southern University's women's team.

In 1992, Harris became the first African-American woman and the first female college player inducted into the Naismith Memorial Basketball Hall of Fame. She was later inducted into the International Women's Sports Hall of Fame, and in 1999, inducted into the inaugural class of the Women's Basketball Hall Fame.

Eugene Bullard

Known as the "Father of African-American Aviators," Eugene Bullard (1895 - 1961) is considered to be the first African-American military pilot to fly in combat, and the only African-American pilot to serve during World War I. Although he was a United States citizen, ironically, he never flew for the United States. When the United States entered the war, American pilots who flew for France were eligible for a U.S. Army commission. Bullard, who had been a member of the French Foreign Legion and the French Army, presented himself to the U.S. Army, but his application was rejected due to his race. He flew twenty combat missions for the French Air Service. Upon his plane he painted the words, "All The Blood That Runs Is Red," a testament to his belief that all men are created equal, regardless of the color of their skin. For his bravery and his daring flights, he was nicknamed the "Black Swallow of Death," and became a highly decorated combat pilot. In 1959, French President Charles de Gaulle made Bullard a Knight of the French Legion of Honor, the nation's highest ranking order and decoration. After forty years of living abroad, Bullard's life in France came to an end with World War II. He returned to America aboard a steamship in 1959. He moved to New York City, where he enthusiastically took part in the French cultural life of the city.

Aviator and decorated war veteran, Eugene Bullard was among the first African-American military pilots in the world. Growing up in Columbus, GA., during the early 1900's, his experience with a Jim Crow segregated South gave him a very unhappy childhood. He was inspired by stories his father told him about France, where a persons social prospect is not limited to their skin color. Unhappy with home life, in 1906 he ran away at the age of eleven. After traveling through the American South for six years, he stowed away aboard a merchant ship in Norfolk, VA., in 1912, which was bound for Europe. After arriving in London, he found employment as a boxer, having 42 professional fights as a lightweight. He decided to reside in Paris after traveling to France in 1913 for a boxing match.

After World War I had begun in the summer of 1914, he enlisted in the French Foreign Legion at the age of nineteen to fight for his adopted country. Bullard served as a machine gunner in his infantry regiment until he was injured in Verdun, France in 1916. Although his wound would take him out of ground combat permanently, his heroism would earn him several military decorations. While recovering from his injury, he learned of the French Flying Service. Bullard was found unfit for the infantry due to his injury, yet he still wanted to get back into the fight, he set his sights on rejoining the war as an aviator.

After rising to the rank of Corporal, he transferred to the French Air Service. He began flight training and received his wings in May 1917, he was then assigned to Escadrille Spa 93. When the United States entered the war in 1917, many American aviators serving with the French transferred to the United States Army Air Service. While Bullard requested a transfer and passed his flight physical, he was denied the opportunity to fly with the Americans due to his race, he served the remainder of the war with the French 170th infantry regiment.

Bullard quickly became known for flying into dangerous situations and proved himself on the battlefield as he was the first African-American combat pilot in WWI. After flying more than twenty combat missions for the French Air Service, he shot down several German planes, his fellow soldiers nicknamed him, the "Black Swallow of Death." He fought with courage and determination in the bloody, grueling Battle of Verdun, where he stayed in the trenches even after suffering a massive head injury. He managed to survive a stretch of fighting that killed thousands of enemy soldiers. Forever a hero in France, he earned a total of fifteen medals. After forty years as a stranger in his own country, he returned to the U.S. in 1959. Finally given the recognition he deserved, the U.S. Military made amends for its treatment of Bullard, he was posthumously granted a commission in the United States Air Force as a 2nd Lieutenant.

Issac Murphy

The most prestigious horse race in America began in 1875, "The Kentucky Derby" which is an annual event scheduled on the first Saturday in May. During its inaugural year, 13 out of the 15 Jockeys were African-American. Isaac Murphy (1861 - 1896) was the first Jockey of any race to win the Kentucky Derby three times, he is also considered the greatest thoroughbred horse rider in American history, winning 44 percent of all of his races. Murphy won his first race in 1884, second in 1890 and third in 1891, which made him the first Jockey to capture Derby titles two years in a row. In 1884, he also became the only Jockey to win the Derby, the Kentucky Oaks and the Clark Stakes in the same Churchill Downs meeting. During the 1820's, horse racing became the most popular sport in the United States, a large number of the best trainers and jockeys in the country were African-Americans. Murphys achievements made him the most famous sports figure in the nation. In 1955, he was the first Jockey voted into the Jockey Hall of Fame at the National Museum of Racing in Saratoga Springs, NY. Organized horse racing dates back to the 17th century in North America. The accomplishments of African-American jockeys in the early years of horse racing are often forgotten, although they were America's first professional athletes.

Hall of Fame jockey, Issac Murphy is considered to be one of the greatest riders in American thoroughbred horse racing history. Born at the dawn of the civil war in 1861, he grew up at a time when horse racing was one of America's most popular sports. Growing up in Lexington, KY., he learned how to ride through a close relationship with his mothers boss, who saw some talent in Murphy, his small stature made him a good prospect as a jockey. In 1875, he won his first race at the age of fourteen.

Murphy began to attract national attention in a race in 1877 in Saratoga, he had a steady hand, a quick eye, and a cool head. His riding style revealed several signature characteristics, most notably his upright riding position. As a rider, he possessed a rare gift for riding thoroughbreds, he understood the horse he was on, and encouraged speed through soft words, not through the whip. He had a knack for keeping his horses calm and developed the technique of the stretch run, he conserved his horse's stamina and sprinted to the finish line while the other horses were wearing down.

Murphy was considered the most dynamic jockey of his era, he was credited as being victorious in an amazing 44 percent of his career races. His first Kentucky Derby win came in 1884, followed by back-to-back wins in 1890 and 1891. He was the first jockey to win that race twice in a row. He also won Chicago's American Derby four times (this race was more prestigious than the Kentucky Derby during the time). He perfected how to pace his horses, winning an astounding 628 times during the course of his career.

He is regarded by many as the greatest jockey of all time due to his record of having the highest winning average than any other jockey in racing history. During the height of his career in the 1880's, Murphy received an average yearly salary of $30,000, making him the highest paid jockey in the United States. Through his natural talent, he gained fame, wealth, and an elite social status that was uncommon for African-Americans during the 19th century. His achievements made him the most famous sports figure in the nation.

When the National Museum of Racing and Hall of Fame opened in Saratoga Springs, N.Y. in 1955, Murphy was the first jockey ever inducted. To honor his career achievements, the National Turf Writers Association now presents the "Isaac Murphy Award" to the jockey in the United States with the highest winning percentage. The Chicago's Arlington International Racecourse also changed the name of its celebrated American Derby to the "Isaac Murphy Stakes."

Dr. Walter Samuel McAfee

Dr. Walter Samuel McAfee (1914 - 1995) is one of the most renowned scientists who served for more than forty years with the Army Signal Corps. As an astronomer and physicist, he is most famous for his pioneering work on "Project Diana" in 1946, which is considered to be the beginning of the Space Age. McAfee and his team participated in successfully calculating the speed of the moon. They sent a radar pulse transmission towards the moon; two and a half seconds later, they received a signal back, proving that transmissions from earth could cross over vast distances into Outer Space. Due to his work and expertise, he put man's imprint on the moon for the first time with radar. His experiment bounced an electronic echo from the moon's surface back to an antenna at the Evans Signal Laboratory, where he was employed as a Physicist in the theoretical studies unit of the Engineering Laboratories, Army Electronics Research Command. McAfee's theoretical calculations determined the feasibility of this original radar "moon bounce." In 1956, President Dwight D. Eisenhower presented him with one of the first Secretary of the Army Research and Study Fellowships. The fellowship enabled McAfee to spend two years studying Radio Astronomy at Harvard University.

Scientist and astronomer, Dr. Walter Samuel McAfee was instrumental in helping to launch the Space Age. Growing up in Ore City, TX., he earned a Bachelor's Degree in Mathematics in 1934 from Wiley College, a Historically Black College and University (HBCU) in Marshall, TX. In 1937, he earned a Master's of Science Degree from Ohio State University. In 1942, McAfee joined the United States Army Signal Corps Engineering Laboratories at Fort Monmouth in Belmar, NJ.

His knowledge and mathematical skillset propelled him to be included on the "Project Diana" team. Project Diana was a scientific collaboration in which engineers studied the earth's relationship to the moon via radar signal echoing. He contributed the necessary theoretical calculations including a radar cross-section of the moon, radar coverage pattern, and the distance to the moon, all of which were crucial to the project's success.

Due to McAfee's work and contribution to the Project, the team successfully received the echoing signals between the earth and the moon on January 10, 1946. After the success of the signal echoing project, he received the Rosenwald Fellowship to continue his Doctoral Degree at Cornell University in Ithaca, N.Y. McAfee then earned his Ph.D. in Physics in 1949, focusing on nuclear collisions.

Upon completion of his Doctoral studies, McAfee rejoined the United States Army Signal Corps Engineering Laboratories at Fort Monmouth as a scientist. He contributed to scientific investigations involving nuclear weapons systems testing and and satellite instrumentation. He was honored with the Secretary of the Army Research and Study Fellowship in 1956 by President Dwight D. Eisenhower, which gave him an opportunity to accept a Post-Doctoral appointment at Harvard University in Cambridge, MA.

McAfee held a number of supervisory positions during his forty years at Fort Monmouth, where he guided the development of new technologies. While working as Director of the Passive Sensing Technical Area in 1966, he directed work on developing acoustic, seismic, magnetic, electromagnetic, and infrared sensors, many of which were used as part of the "McNamara Line" to detect and track enemy movements during the war in Vietnam. While recognized for his scientific accomplishments, service to country, and commitment to academic excellence, McAfee was inducted into the Science Hall of Fame in 1982 at his alma mater, Wiley College. In 2015, McAfee became the first African-American inducted into the Army Materiel Command's Hall of Fame.

Colonel Allen Allensworth

Colonel Allen Allensworth (1842 - 1914) was the first African-American to reach the rank of Lieutenant-Colonel in the United States Army. While serving in the military, Allensworth discovered that of the four African-American Army regiments (the Buffalo Soldiers) there were no African-American Chaplains, he immediately sought that appointment. On April 1, 1886, President Grover Cleveland appointed him as Chaplain of the 24th Infantry at the rank of Captain, with the responsibility for the spiritual health and educational well-being of African-American soldiers in the regiment. After serving in the Army for twenty years, he retired in 1906 as a Lieutenant-Colonel, having achieved the highest rank of an African-American in the U.S. Armed Forces during the time. Allensworth and his family then settled in Los Angeles, CA. He was inspired by the idea of establishing a self-sufficient California community where African-Americans could live free of the racial discrimination which eluded post-Reconstruction America. In 1908, he established the first all African-American township named "Allensworth," which is thirty miles North of Bakersfield. Allensworth was sanctioned as a Judicial District by the state in 1914. Along with residents, the town had several businesses including a barber shop, bakery, theater, drug store, and the Allensworth Hotel. Today the site is known as "Colonel Allensworth State Historic Park."

Union soldier, Baptist minister and educator who created his own township, Allen Allensworth was the highest ranking African-American in the U.S. military in the early 20th century. Growing up enslaved in Louisville, KY., he was sent to live with a Quaker family as a young child. He learned how to read and write while attending schools for enslaved children as he moved around often throughout his teenage years.

At the age of twenty, Allensworth traveled to Louisville for a horse race where he met Union Soldiers from the 44th Illinois Volunteer Infantry Regiment who were in the area. When he expressed his longing for freedom, the soldiers invited him to join their Hospital Corps. As the infantry was ready to depart Louisville, the soldiers loaned him a Union coat. His newfound friends encircled him as he was disguised as one of their own, and Allensworth was able to get out of town without detection, ending his time of slavery.

Allensworth remained with the 44th infantry as a nursing aide for a several years and then enlisted in the U.S. Navy. After the civil war ended, he attended Roger Williams University in Nashville to study Theology, where he also met and married Josephine Leavell, a music teacher and pianist. The two moved back to Louisville where Allensworth oversaw the work of several churches.

During the early 1880's, many African-American soldiers approached Allensworth to discuss a problem. While the U.S. military maintained two cavalry and two infantry units of African-Americans, the soldiers had no chaplain. Allensworth took the plea seriously. After writing letters to members of Congress as well as President Grover Cleveland for two years, his appointment was confirmed by the Senate, and approved by the President in 1886, an assignment he maintained for twenty years. Shortly before his retirement, Allensworth was promoted to the rank of Lieutenant-Colonel, making him the first African-American officer to receive this rank.

After he retired, Allensworth and his family settled in Los Angeles. Troubled by the societal issues of the early 20th century, as it was an era of segregation and discrimination, he envisioned a town built with the intention of establishing a self-sufficient city where African-Americans could create a better life for themselves outside of a segregated U.S. society. In 1908, he established the first all African-American township named Allensworth, CA. Agriculture dominated the economy as several farmers moved into the township. In 1912, Allensworth had a voting precinct and its own school district encompassing thirty square miles, during its peak in the 1920's, Allensworth had a population of several hundred residents.

Frederick D. "Fritz" Pollard

Frederick Douglass "Fritz" Pollard (1894 - 1986) was a pioneer in professional football in more ways than one. He led Brown University to the 1916 Rose Bowl. The 5'9" 165-pound running-back was the first African-American to play in the prestigious game and the second to receive All-American honors in college football. Once Pollard left Brown, University, he signed a contract to play for the "Akron Pros" in 1919, following army service during World War I. He was an exciting elusive runner who was the most feared running-back in the league. In 1920, the Pros joined the newly founded American Professional Football League (APFA), which was later renamed the National Football League (NFL). As a member of the new league, Pollard immediately earned a place in professional football history as one of just two African-Americans in the new league. In 1921, he earned another distinction becoming the first African-American head coach in NFL history when the Pros named him coach of the team. Pollard was the highest paid player in the league earning $1,500 a game during the 1920's. Among his many honors, he was posthumously inducted into the Pro Football Hall of Fame in 2005. Pollard was also the first African-American to be elected into the National College Football Hall of Fame and the first recipient of an Honorary Doctorate Degree from Brown University. Along with his amazing athletic ability and accomplishments, Pollard was an advocate for confronting racial barriers and creating opportunities for African-Americans, both in the athletic and business world.

American football player and coach, Frederick Douglass "Fritz" Pollard was one of the earliest stars of professional football. Born in an affluent neighborhood in Chicago, IL., he was affectionately called Fred, but later nicknamed "Fritz" by neighborhood residents, a name that stuck with him throughout his life. He was however named after activist and author, Frederick Douglass, a famous abolitionist whom his parents heard speak many times prior to his birth. By the time he graduated from Lane Technical High School in 1912, he had become a talented running-back. In 1915, he received a Rockefeller Scholarship to attend Brown University in Providence, RI.

Pollard was a highly successful football and track athlete, as a freshman running-back at Brown during the 1916 football season, he was nicknamed "the human torpedo," as he single-handedly defeated other Ivy League University's including Yale and Harvard. He scored 12 touchdowns for the season and led Brown to an 8-1 record, gaining notoriety as the first African-American to ever play in the Rose Bowl. He also set a world record for Browns track and field team and qualified for the U.S. Olympic Team. After college he became head coach of Lincoln University in Pennsylvania in 1918.

After serving in World War I, Pollard joined the Akron Pros in 1919, which in 1920 joined the American Professional Football Association (APFA), later being renamed the National Football League (NFL). The Akron Pros went undefeated during Pollard's first season, winning the leagues first NFL Championship. He also facilitated integration in the NFL by recruiting other African-American players as well as organizing the first interracial all-star game featuring NFL players. In 1921, Pollard became the first African-American head coach in the NFL. He made history once again in 1923 as the first African-American quarterback in the NFL. He was also an exciting elusive runner, which made him the most feared running-back in the league.

As an athlete, he became a symbol of a new generation of African-Americans who emerged as pioneers in breaking down color barriers. Pollard's experiences on the football field led him in his post-playing years to a lifetime commitment toward African-American advancement in other areas such as business, entertainment, and journalism. In 1935, Pollard founded his own professional football team, the "Brown Bombers." The team was extremely popular and successful until the Great Depression ended their run in 1938. He then explored other ventures, including film and music production. In 2005, he was posthumously inducted into the Pro Football Hall of Fame. He was also inducted into the Rose Bowl Hall of Fame in 2015.

Septima Poinsette Clark

As a pioneer in grassroots citizenship education, Septima Poinsette Clark (1898 - 1987) was often called the "Mother of the Movement" and the epitome of a community leader and fighter for civil rights. Clark developed the literacy and citizenship workshops that played an important role in the drive for voting rights. African-American men and women had the right to vote, but were often kept from the voting polls by literacy tests. Many could not read due to their parents and grandparents being formerly enslaved. Slavery was legal in the United States until 1863, and it was illegal to teach an enslaved person how to read and write. As a result, literacy tests prevented many African-American citizens from voting, even in the 1950's and 1960's. As a South Carolina school teacher, Clark wanted to do more to advance the rights of African-Americans, she joined the Charleston branch of the National Association for the Advancement of Colored People (NAACP). She later joined the Southern Christian Leadership Conference (SCLC) in 1961 as Director of Education and Teaching. In 1962, the SCLC joined with other organizations to form the "Voter Education Project,"which trained teachers through "Citizenship Schools." This led to increased voter registrations among African-Americans citizens. A decade later, over two-million African-Americans became registered voters due to Clark's dedication to the movement. As a result, the first African-Americans since reconstruction were elected to the U.S. Congress.

Educator and civil rights activist, Septima Poinsette Clark pioneered the link between education and political organizing. Growing up in Charleston, S.C., her life was greatly affected by the era of reconstruction, the city was strictly segregated and harshly divided by class. Her early experience of racial discrimination fueled her pursuit of racial equality, and led to a commitment to strengthen the African-American community through literacy and citizenship.

In 1916, she graduated from high school, she then passed her teacher's exam and taught at an African-American school on Johns Island, just outside of Charleston. She taught throughout South Carolina for more than thirty years, including eighteen years in Columbia and nine years in Charleston. Clark pursued higher education during summer breaks. In 1937, she studied under W. E. B. Du Bois at Atlanta University before eventually earning her B.A. from Benedict College in 1942, and her M.A. from Hampton Institute in 1946.

During this time, she was active in several social and civic organizations, among them the National Association for the Advancement of Colored People (NAACP). She also joined the Southern Christian Leadership Conference (SCLC) in 1961, as Director of Education and Teaching. She developed the concept of "Citizenship Education," which was designed to help African-American adults pass the literacy test that was required for voting in elections. This was an integral part of the effort to educate African-Americans about the rights they had as United States citizens so they could vigorously assert these rights in the fight against segregation.

This became the cornerstone of the civil rights movement, which wanted to grant rights for African-Americans throughout the country. Clarke also worked closely with Dr. Martin Luther King, Jr., who commonly referred to her as "The Mother of the Movement." In 1962, the SCLC joined with other organizations to form the "Voter Education Project," which was designed to aid literacy programs and foster a sense of political empowerment within the African-American community. As a result, over two-million African-Americans became new registered voters.

Clark believed in the power of literacy and non-violent resistance, she was not only teaching literacy, but also citizenship rights. Her goals for the schools were to provide self-pride, cultural-pride, literacy, and a sense of one's citizenship rights. In 1979, President Jimmy Carter honored her with a "Living Legacy Award." Clark's argument for her position in the civil rights movement was one that claimed, "Knowledge Could Empower Marginalized Groups In ways that Formal Legal Equality Couldn't."

Dr. Samuel Lee Kountz

Dr. Samuel Lee Kountz (1930 - 1981) was the first doctor in the United States to perform a successful kidney transplant between humans who were not identical twins. He later developed the prototype for the Belzer Kidney Perfusion Machine, a device that can preserve kidneys for up to 50 hours from the time they are taken from a donor's body. This device is now standard equipment in hospitals and research laboratories around the world. Kountz later helped develop a number of new techniques in transplantation and greatly advanced the accuracy and sophistication of tissue-typing tests that are crucial to the success of transplant operations. In an era where the high cost of transplantation made it unavailable to the urban poor, and African-American community, Kountz used his fame to support federal funding for treatment to end kidney disease, including kidney transplantation. As part of his campaign to increase awareness of the need for living donors in kidney transplantation, Kountz went on "The Today Show" to perform the first live kidney transplant on television in 1975. After its airing, he inspired 20,000 viewers to serve as living donors and offer their kidneys to patients who needed them. In addition, his groundbreaking research in the area of tissue typing helped improve the results of kidney transplantation and led to the increased use of kidneys from unrelated donors worldwide.

Renowned surgeon and pioneer in organ transplants, Samuel Lee Kountz was one of the world's most distinguished surgeons in the field of kidney transplantation. He was raised in the town of Lexa, AR., which was one of the most impoverished areas in the state in the 1930's. Without a doctor in the town, Kountz's father often assumed the role of nurse and his mother was a midwife. His parents work inspired him to become a physician.

Kountz was one of the first African-American students to graduate from the University of Arkansas Medical School in Little Rock, he then went on to complete his medical training at Stanford University. While still a resident, he established a special organ transplant unit. While training at the Stanford Medical Center, Kountz discovered that large doses of methylprednisolone stopped the rejection of transplanted kidneys. In addition, he performed the first kidney transplant between patients who were not identical twins in 1964.

This groundbreaking transplant between a mother and daughter, made future kidney transplants possible for thousands of patients. In the following eight years, 5000 kidney transplants were performed. Kountz later became chief of the Kidney Transplant Service at the University of California, San Francisco. While at the university in 1967, he produced a machine capable of preserving donated human kidneys for more than two days while they were delivered to a suitable recipient.

In 1972, he left California to accept a position of Professor and Chairperson of the Department of Surgery at the State University of New York's Downstate Medical Center in Brooklyn. Although he had been offered a number of prestigious positions across the country, he chose Downstate which was situated in the heart of a predominantly African-American area of Brooklyn.

Driven by a deep social consciousness and a commitment to humanity, Kountz spent most of his career working to improve medical care in the African-American community. In addition, he succeeded in turning Downstate's organ transplant program into one of the best in the country, he wasted no time in recruiting new staff, establishing research priorities, and improving the hospital's residency program. In 1976, he made medical history once again when he and his surgical team performed a successful kidney transplant on a three month old child named, Alexandra Kelly, who became the world's youngest and smallest transplant patient in history.

Jane Bolin

Jane Bolin (1908 - 2007) shattered several glass ceilings during her career. As a trailblazing attorney, she was the first African-American woman Judge in the United States, serving on New York's Family Court for four decades. She broke through several barriers during her life including becoming the first African-American woman to graduate from Yale Law School and the first to gain admission to the New York City Bar. Bolin used her position from the bench to fight against racial discrimination within the legal system, she also used her authority to defend justice and equality for women. She was a fierce advocate for children, particularly children of color, whose cases she oversaw. One of her many accomplishments as a Family Court Judge was changing the system so that publicly funded child care agencies had to accept children without discriminating on race or ethnicity. During her tenure, she worked closely alongside First Lady Eleanor Roosevelt to decrease juvenile crimes among young boys nationwide. For over twenty years, Bolin was the only African-American woman judge in the United States, beyond the courtroom, she was an outspoken and staunch advocate for civil rights.

Educator and scholar, Jane Bolin was a true pioneer in the judicial field, growing up in Poughkeepsie, New York, she was an outstanding student, graduating from high school at the age of fifteen. Her passion for advocacy and social justice emerged during her childhood. Having been exposed to the plight of African-American people while growing up, she was determined to pursue a career in law. Bolin believed that in the field of law, she would be able to achieve great advances for the African-American community.

After graduating Wellesley College in Massachusetts, she successfully enrolled at Yale Law School and became the first African-American woman to earn a Law Degree from the institution at the age of twenty-three, as well as becoming the first to pass the New York state bar examination in 1932. In 1939, New York City Mayor Fiorello La Guardia appointed Bolin as a Family Court Judge, making her the first African-American woman judge in the United States.

Bolin devoted herself and her passion for law to advocating specifically for civil service, civil rights, children's rights, and education. She made many substantial changes to ensure that children of color could receive necessary public funds, she spent countless years working on domestic cases. Her tireless fight behind the scenes allowed her to also work alongside First Lady Eleanor Roosevelt, together they helped create an intervention program to help guide young boys from committing crimes.

During her tenure as a judge, Bolin achieved two legal landmarks, she eliminated the assignments of probation officers based on ethnicity, and she mandatorily made private child-care agencies, which ran on public funds, help children regardless of their background. She was responsible for transforming massive elements of the family court system. Bolin's original ten year term as a judge was reconfirmed by three New York City Mayors which extended her judgeship by forty years. Half of her career on the bench she remained Americas only African-American woman judge.

Having achieved her childhood dream of making a difference, Bolin actively avoided consideration for other positions that would have taken her away from this area of the court. When she retired after forty years of service on the bench, she continued to work on behalf of children's welfare, she spent two years volunteering in New York City public schools as a reading and math instructor. She has been sighted by many African-American women in law as a trailblazer and major inspiration to them. Throughout her career, she also served on the board of the NAACP and New York Urban League.

John Steward Rock

On February 1, 1865, the day after the House of Representatives passed the 13th Amendment which abolished slavery, John Steward Rock (1825 - 1866) was the first African-American ever admitted to practice law before the Supreme Court of the United States. For Rock, who was associated with coining the term "Black is Beautiful," had already won acclaim as a teacher, dentist, and doctor all before turning thirty years old, it was the latest in a long list of accomplishments. As a doctor, Rock lived in Boston, MA., in 1853, which was considered the most liberal city in the United States for African-Americans during the time. There he set up his own practice in dentistry and medicine. Many of his patients turned out to be formally enslaved people who made their way through Boston on the underground railroad, fleeing towards Canada. Rock increasingly identified with the abolitionist movement and soon became a prominent speaker for that cause. While he called on the United States government to end slavery, he also urged African-Americans to use their talents and resources to assist their communities. Over the next several years he rose to even greater heights, emerging as a leader in Boston's free African-American community and winning national recognition as a reform lecturer. Education and economic improvement were vital to his vision for a new America. He believed true equality would be achieved only when African-Americans were given economic power. He was a part of the National Equal Rights League along with other famous abolitionists such as Frederick Douglass and John Mercer Langston.

Educator, dentist, physician, and attorney, John S. Rock was one of the leading abolitionist in New England in the mid-19th century, he was a prolific orator and is credited with coining the term "Black is Beautiful." Growing up in Salem, NJ., in the 1830's, his parents supported him having the best education. In 1844, at the age of nineteen, Rock was fluent in greek and latin, he then accepted a teaching position at an African-American public grammar school in Salem.

Although he enjoyed teaching, he deeply desired to become a doctor, studying nights in the hopes of gaining admission to medical school. He apprenticed with two local doctors, Dr. Shaw and Dr. Gibson. After four years of teaching and apprenticeship, he prepared to enter medical school. However, because he was African-American, no medical school would admit him. Discouraged but not ready to give up his dream completely, Rock began studying dentistry. During the time, an academic degree was not required to practice dentistry.

He found a job working for a local dentist, who was so impressed with Rock's intellect that he made him his apprentice. In 1849, after a year learning the dental profession, Rock decided to establish his own practice in Philadelphia, which had one of the country's largest populations of free African-Americans. Determined not to give up his dream on becoming a doctor, he re-applied and was accepted to Philadelphia's American Medical College and received his Medical Degree at the age of twenty-six.

In 1853, Rock then moved to Boston to open a medical and dental office. Boston was the home of a well-organized, influential group of African-American leaders and a hotbed for the abolitionist movement. After setting up his business in Boston, he began giving many speeches on racial issues that earned him public notice. He was a passionate abolitionist and civil rights leader and held a strong belief in the dignity and rights of all Americans. By 1855, he traveled extensively throughout New England to deliver public lectures. Due to his many years of work and public service, he then became chronically ill and his doctors recommended he give up his stressful careers.

Although maybe not what his doctors had in mind, Rock closed his medical and dentistry practices and decided to become a lawyer, he then set his sights on a milestone achievement. Perhaps one of his greatest marks in history, in 1865, he became the first African-American to gain admittance and argue a case before the U.S. Supreme Court. The day after this unprecedented event, Rock was then received by the U.S. House of Representatives, and he became the first African-American lawyer to be introduced at a session of congress.

Howard Thurman

Howard Thurman (1899 - 1991) was one of the most celebrated
religious figures of the 20th century. He was a reserved man who
didn't lead marches or give dramatic speeches, but he was a spiritual
genius who transformed history. After having a historic meeting with
Mohandas Gandhi in the 1930's, Thurman became one of the early
voices of non-violent resistance in combating racial inequality. In 1944
he founded Fellowship Church in San Francisco, CA., this was the first
congregation in the United States that encouraged participation in its
spiritual life regardless of religious or ethnic background. As a prominent
religious figure and a spiritual mentor to Dr. Martin Luther King Jr., he
played a leading role in many social justice movements and organizations
during the 1950's and 1960's. Thurman's theology of radical non-violence
influenced shaped a generation of civil rights activists. As a pastor and
teacher, he provided a spiritual perspective that was empowering, his
groundbreaking book, "Jesus and the Disinherited," revolutionized
the traditional portrait of Jesus Christ and had a profound influence
on Dr. Martin Luther King Jr.'s faith and activism.

Author, educator, and civil rights leader, Howard Thurman is often referred to as one of the 50 most important figures in African-American history. Growing up in Daytona Beach, FL., in the early 1900's, his family stressed education as a means of overcoming racial discrimination. In 1923, he graduated as valedictorian from Morehouse College in Atlanta, GA., with a Bachelor of Arts Degree in Economics. After graduation, he became ordained as a Baptist Minister in 1925.

He then served as pastor of a Baptist Church in Oberlin, OH., and pursued graduate course work in theology at Oberlin College. In 1932, he was selected as the first Dean of Rankin Chapel at Howard University in Washington, D.C. In 1944, he left Howard and founded Fellowship Church in San Francisco, CA., this was the first congregation in the United States that encouraged participation in its spiritual life regardless of religious or ethnic background.

Thurman remained at the church until 1953, he then assumed the Deanship of Boston University's Marsh Chapel. He was very active and well known in the Boston community, where he influenced many local leaders. Thurman taught many prominent students at the university including Dr. Martin Luther King, Jr. He would later serve as a spiritual mentor to Dr. King and several other future civil rights leaders.

Thurman often traveled abroad, heading Christian missions and meeting with world figures such as Mahatma Gandhi. When Thurman asked Gandhi what message should he take back to America, Gandhi replied "I regret not having made non-violence more visible worldwide," and suggested some African-American man would succeed where he had failed. Gandhi instilled within Thurman an appreciation for the value of non-violent resistance in combating racial inequality.

Prior to the civil rights movement, Dr. Martin Luther King, Jr., read from Thurman's book "Jesus and the Disinherited." This book laid much of the philosophical foundation for non-violent resistance during the civil rights movement. According to Thurman, fear, deception, and hatred prohibits a peaceful end to racial bigotry. By the time the civil rights movement took shape in the United States, Thurman was a nationally recognized human rights advocate, though he did not take to marching and mobilizing on the streets. He preferred to serve as a caretaker and spiritual advisor to those who did, among them Dr. Martin Luther King, Jr., Jesse Jackson, and Marian Wright Edelman.

Susie King Taylor

Susie King Taylor (1848 - 1912) achieved many firsts in her lifetime, many of her contributions during the civil war impacted the future of the United States. During the war, Taylor and thousands of other African-Americans found themselves seeking safety behind the Union Army lines on the South Carolina Sea Islands. She soon attached herself to an African-American army regiment named the First South Carolina Volunteers, later renamed the 33rd United States Colored Infantry Regiment, where her husband served for four years during the civil war. She served the Union Army in various capacities, officially as a laundress, but in reality a nurse, and educator. Her literacy proved most useful and enabled her to serve as a teacher for the regiment of former enslaved people. In 1866, she established a school for newly freed African-American children. By the early 1870's, she moved to Boston, MA., where she joined and then became President of the Women's Relief Corps, a national organization for female civil war veterans which gave assistance to soldiers and hospitals. In 1902, she published these experiences in her book, "Reminiscences of My Life in Camp," she was the only African-American woman to publish a memoir of her wartime experiences during the civil war. By the turn of the 20th century, as Jim Crow laws and violence toward African-Americans escalated, Taylor became an outspoken racial justice activist, she stood firm against racial prejudice and discrimination.

Teacher and nurse, Susie King Taylor is a woman of great significance to the state of Georgia and the nations history. Born enslaved in Liberty County, GA., she lived on a plantation. As a young girl, she knew the importance of learning how to read and write, and would let no one get in the way of her being taught. At the age of seven, she was allowed an opportunity to move to Savannah and live with her grandmother who was free. Every morning her grandmother allowed her to attend a nearby school in secret, it was a very dangerous journey for them as there were harsh laws against the formal education of African-Americans, however they were willing to take that risk for the sake of education.

In 1862, Fort Pulaski at the mouth of the Savannah River fell to Union troops. As the Union Army took a firm hold of the South Carolina and Georgia coasts, thousands of enslaved people escaped to seek refuge with Union troops. Shortly after, Union officers learned that Taylor was educated. They offered to provide her books and materials if she would start a school and teach the illiterate children and adults at the camp how to read and write.

At the age of fourteen, Taylor founded the first African-American school for formally enslaved children, she also became the first African-American woman to teach a school in the state of Georgia. By day, she taught children, and at night, she taught their parents. In 1863, Taylor married Edward King, an enslaved carpenter from Darien, GA., who had escaped to volunteer for the U.S. Army. His unit was renamed the 33rd Regiment United States Colored Infantry Regiment after the Emancipation Proclamation officially allowed African-American men to serve in the U.S. Army.

Taylor enrolled as an army laundress and traveled with her husband's regiment, apart from working as a teacher to the men, she also served as a nurse. She tended those wounded in battle, but also cared for anyone who had contracted smallpox since she had already been vaccinated. In 1866, Edward King was killed in a work accident, leaving a pregnant Taylor widowed. Continuing her work as a teacher, she moved to Boston where she met and married Russell L. Taylor in 1879.

Taylor then devoted herself to veteran's aid projects. She helped organize Corps 67 Women's Relief Corps, a support branch of the Grand Army of the Republic (GAR). Serving as the President of the GAR, she decided to write her memoirs. Published in 1902, "Reminiscences of My Life in Camp," Taylor was the only African-American woman to publish a memoir of her wartime experiences, her significant contributions to the civil war were undeniable and monumental.

Charles Hamilton Houston

Charles Hamilton Houston (1895 - 1950) exposed the hollowness of the "separate but equal" doctrine and paved the way for the Supreme Court ruling to outlaw school segregation. He played a significant role in dismantling Jim Crow laws, especially attacking segregation in schools and racial housing covenants across the country, earning the title "The Man Who Killed Jim Crow." During the 1930's and 1940's, he served as the first general counsel for the National Association for the Advancement of Colored People (NAACP), arguing several important civil rights cases before the U.S. Supreme Court. He traveled through the South in the early 1930's and noted the inequalities of African-American school facilities. In response, they developed the legal strategy which challenged school segregation, first calling for the equalization of facilities for African-American students and then eventually calling for full integration. Also serving as Dean of Howard University Law School, he shaped it into a significant institution. The school trained one-fourth of the nation's African-American law students, among them Thurgood Marshall. During Houston's tenure, the school became accredited by the Association of American Law Schools and the American Bar Association. Houston later worked closely with his student and mentee Marshall, together they laid the groundwork for the landmark 1954 case, Brown vs. Board of Education, declaring the "separate but equal" notion was unconstitutional.

Attorney, Dean of Howard University Law School, and NAACP Special Counsel, Charles Hamilton Houston made significant contributions in the battle against racial discrimination, and challenging several Jim Crow laws. Growing up in Washington D.C. he attended Amherst College in Massachusetts where he was valedictorian and the only African-American student of their graduating class in 1915. After graduation, he taught English at Historically Black College and University (HBCU) Howard University before joining the U.S. Army in WWI.

Houston's experience in the racially segregated U.S. Army, where he served as a First Lieutenant in France made him determined to study law and use his time to fight for men and women who were discriminated against. He returned to the U.S. in 1919 and entered Harvard Law School, becoming the first African-American student to be elected to the Editorial Board of the Harvard Law Review. After graduating from Harvard with a Doctor of Laws Degree in 1923, he was admitted to the District of Columbia bar and joined forces with his father in practicing law. He once again joined the staff at Howard University.

As the Dean of the Howard University Law School, Houston expanded the part-time program into a full-time curriculum. He also mentored a generation of young African-American lawyers, including Thurgood Marshall, who would go on to become a United States Supreme Court Justice. Due to the American Bar Association's refusal of access to African-American members, Houston became one of the founding members of the National Bar Association in 1925, which is an organization for African-American attorneys and judges.

In the mid-1930's, Houston began his legal battle to end segregation in public education. He planned his strategy on three different levels. First, he argued that inequality existed in the educational opportunities of African-American and Caucasian students. Second, he claimed that inequality was too expensive for states to maintain, and finally, he attacked the "separate but equal" principle upon which segregation rested. His ingenious legal strategy was to end school segregation by unmasking the belief that African-American facilities were equal, his strategy worked effectively paving the way for desegregation. Houston then left Howard University to serve as the first General Counsel of the NAACP.

He played a pivotal role in nearly every supreme court civil rights case prior to the landmark Brown vs. Board of Education ruling in 1954, he worked tirelessly to fight against Jim Crow laws that prevented African-Americans from serving on juries and accessing housing. The legal brilliance used to undercut the "separate but equal" principle earned Houston the title, "The Man Who Killed Jim Crow."

Charlotte E. Ray

In 1872, Charlotte E. Ray (1850 - 1911) was the first African-American woman in the United States to become an Attorney, she was also the first woman admitted to practice before the Supreme Court of the District of Columbia. She was admitted to the Howard University School of Law, due to gender discrimination she used an alternate name (C. E. Ray) to disguise her gender so that her admission would not be instantly revoked. During the 19th century, women were largely barred from the legal profession. They were forbidden from obtaining licenses to practice law and couldn't join the professional associations that would allow them to advance in their careers. As just one of three women in the country who practiced law, Ray opened her own law office and ran advertisements in a newspaper ran by abolitionist, Frederick Douglass. She was also involved in the women's suffrage movement, joining the newly formed organization "National Association of Colored Women." Although racial and gender discrimination forced her to close her law office after practicing for a few years, Ray demonstrated that African-American women could excel in the field of law, her monumental achievements helped to inspire future generations of aspiring attorneys. Since 1989, Ray has been recognized by the Washington D.C. Chapter of Women Lawyers of the National Bar Association, the organization awards an outstanding African-American woman attorney annually with the Charlotte E. Ray Award.

Educator and pioneer, Charlotte E. Ray was not only the first African-American woman attorney in the United States, but she was also the first woman to practice in the District of Columbia, and the third American woman of any race to earn a Law Degree. Growing up in New York City during the 1850's, her father Charles Ray was a pastor and an abolitionist newspaper editor, and her mother Charlotte Ray helped many enslaved people escape North on the underground railroad. Together they made sure their seven children had a quality education.

After her family relocated to Washington D.C., Ray attended one of the few schools in the country that educated African-American girls, which was the Myrtilla Miner Institution for the Education of Colored Youth. After graduating in 1869, she accepted a teaching position at Historically Black College and University (HBCU) Howard University, just two years after the school was established. Howard was one of the few places in America that a formal education for African-Americans was even possible during the time. Although she enjoyed teaching, her ambition was to become an attorney.

She was then accepted into the Howard School of Law, where she applied under the name "C.E. Ray," due to the university being reluctant to admit women to its law program. Ray earned her Law Degree in 1872 and was admitted to the District of Columbia Bar that same year. She then opened a law practice in Washington, D.C., specializing in commercial law. To attract clients, she advertised in a newspaper called "The New National Era and Citizen" which was owned by Frederick Douglass, a prominent African-American abolitionist.

One of her most recognized cases was her representation of Martha Gadley, an African-American woman who petitioned for divorce from her husband. Gadley's petition was denied in 1875, but Ray agreed to take the case on appeal to the District of Columbia's Supreme Court. She successfully overturned the lower court's ruling. Despite her success, Ray was unable to obtain sufficient cases for representation, it was difficult to attract enough clients to maintain an active practice. Racial and gender discrimination forced her to close her office.

In 1879, she returned to New York City to work as a teacher in the Brooklyn public school system. As a pioneer, her contributions to law are celebrated annually with two awards made in her honor, The Annual Charlotte E. Ray Award from the Washington D. C. Area Chapter of Women Lawyers of the National Bar Association, and the MCCA Charlotte E. Ray Award, presented to a woman attorney for her exceptional achievements in the legal profession and extraordinary contribution to the advancement of women in the profession.

Dr. James McCune Smith

Opportunities of freedom, education, and access to healthcare were often out of reach for African-Americans during the early 1800's. Dr. James McCune Smith (1814 - 1865) pioneered a path towards a groundbreaking achievement of becoming the first known African-American to earn a Medical Degree in the United States. After studying at the African Free School in New York City, no American university would admit him due to his race. He then travelled to Scotland and graduated at the top of his class from the University of Glasgow in 1837. After returning home to New York as a medical doctor, he was greeted as a hero by the African-American community. Smith was also the first African-American to run a pharmacy in the United States. In addition to practicing as a doctor for twenty years, he contributed articles to medical journals. He drew from his medical training to discredit popular misconceptions about differences among the races. Smith was an avid abolitionist and supporter of the underground railroad. As a member of the American Anti-Slavery Society, he helped Frederick Douglass establish the "National Council of Colored People" in 1853, which was the first national organization for African-Americans in the nation. Douglass often stated Smith was "The Single Most Important Influence In His Life." He was a trailblazer and champion for economic and social justice. During the 1850's, he organized committees in New York City to resist the newly passed "Fugitive Slave Law," he also provided medical care and aid to enslaved people on the underground railroad.

Activist, writer, doctor and intellectual, James McCune Smith was one of the most prominent and influential African-Americans during the 1800's. Born enslaved in New York City, he was set free in 1827 at the age of fourteen by the Emancipation Act of New York. Growing up in Manhattan, he later attended the African Free School where he excelled as an exceptional student. He applied to several university medical programs in the U.S. and was denied admission due to his race. Many local abolitionists joined together to financially support Smith and his desire to study medicine.

He chased his dream across the ocean, attending the University of Glasgow in Scotland. He earned his Bachelor's, Masters, and Medical Degree by the age of twenty-four. He graduated with honors and was immediately given a prestigious clinical residency in Glasgow's Lock Hospital. Smith became the first African-American to be published in a British Medical Journal. When he returned to New York City in 1837, he established his own medical office and pharmacy at 93 West Broadway, making him the first university-trained African-American physician with his own practice in the United States. He specialized in general surgery and family medicine, he treated both African-American and Caucasian patients.

He worked there for twenty years trying to protect his community by regularly giving vaccinations for smallpox. Although he was a highly respected and successful physician, he was also an advocate for social justice. His work in the abolitionist movement was unparalleled, he put the needs of his community before the advancement of his own career. Smith worked closely with Frederick Douglass to establish the "National Council of Colored People." Smith had a major influence in the life of Douglass, he was also well known for writing the introduction to Douglass book "My Bondage and My Freedom," the second edition of his autobiography that was published in 1855. He also co-founded the interracial Radical Abolitionist Party along with Douglass in 1855.

Often referred to as the foremost African-American intellectual of the 19th century, he was fluent in French, German, Greek, Hebrew, Italian, Latin, and Spanish, he also authored more than 100 articles in medicine. His lifelong commitment to abolitionism brought him state and national recognition. Smith publicly defied the 1850 Fugitive Slave Act, which required that citizens in free States aid in the recapture of enslaved people fleeing bondage. As he met with other African-American activists in the back room of his pharmacy, they arranged protection for runaways. From the early 1840's, he provided leadership for the campaign to expand African-American voting rights in New York City.

Philip Anthony Payton, Jr.

Harlem, New York is world renowned for being an epicenter of African-American culture and art. The concentration of African-American residents in Harlem is primarily due to real estate mogul Philip Anthony Payton Jr. (1876 - 1917). By the 1890's, sections of the community were lined with four-story brownstone row houses and the area was known as a prosperous residential neighborhood. In 1900, construction began on a subway line extending New York City from lower Manhattan to North 145th Street in Harlem. Real estate developers responded to the construction by building apartment houses in close proximity to the line. Payton recognized an opportunity for African-Americans in these developments. The African-American community in New York began to grow substantially as they relocated from Southern states to New York for better opportunities. Payton's real estate business was incorporated in 1904 as the "Afro-American Realty Company," he acquired leases on hundreds of Harlem properties with a plan of renting to African-American residents. He conceived the idea while attending the annual meeting of Booker T. Washington's National Negro Business League. The African-American movement to Harlem continued throughout the first half of the 20th century, Payton played a significant role in the racial transition of the neighborhood. Harlem was occupied by African-American residents and businesses, setting the stage for the Harlem Renaissance of the 1920's, the community then became known as the "Negro Capital of the World."

Entrepreneur and businessman, who is commonly referred to as the "Father of Harlem," Philip A. Payton Jr. is one of the primary real estate developers responsible for opening up Harlem, New York for African-American settlement in the early 20th century. While growing up in Westfield, MA., Payton was surrounded by an accomplished family who were skilled in many forms of trade, he dropped out of high school during his senior year due to a football injury. He then decided to follow his father's trade and worked as a barber.

During the end of the 19th century, the number of African-Americans migrating from the South to New York City was growing, nearly doubling from 1880 to 1890. In 1899, Payton moved to New York, he worked a series of jobs before eventually finding work as a porter in a real estate office. As he was exposed to the inner workings of the real estate profession, in less than a year he learned first hand the entire profession and decided to start his own real estate company in 1904. After four years of hard work, and convincing property owners to sell to him, his business the "Afro-American Realty Company" began to thrive.

Within three years, the company owned more than 25 buildings and had more than 1,500 tenants under management in Harlem. Payton appealed for help from the city's African-American business community, mostly dominated by members of the National Negro Business League, consisting of the city's leading African-American businessmen. Due to his real estate investments, the African-American population in Harlem grew to over 80,000 residents. Payton enabled generations of African-American New Yorkers to live in prime areas in Manhattan.

Along with managing modern homes which were close to nearby parks and free from racial violence, he became a crusading capitalist who believed the free market was the key to combating racial segregation. Recognized as the most successful real estate developer in the country, Payton played a central role in Harlem's transformation. He later closed his largest deal in 1917, selling six apartment buildings for over $1.5 million, which was the largest sale of housing for African-Americans in the city during the time.

The buildings were renamed after prominent African-American historical figures such as Booker T. Washington, Crispus Attucks, Phyllis Wheatley, Paul Laurence Dunbar, and Frederick Douglass. Continuing his work in real estate, he started a new firm, the "Philip A. Payton Company," which owned and managed buildings in Harlem and were identified by signs displaying his company logo "PAP," which were his initials. The company had a capitalization of $2 million, making it one of the largest African-American owned enterprises in the country during the time.

Ophelia DeVore

Businesswoman, Ophelia DeVore (1922 - 2014) is the first African-American Model in the United States, she enrolled in the Vogue School of Modeling at the age of seventeen. DeVore modeled for several years before deciding to help other African-American women overcome stereotypes and succeed in the field. In 1946, she helped establish the Grace Del Marco Agency, one of the first modeling agencies in America. The Agency was the entry point for a number of future models and actors including Diahann Carrol, Helen Williams, Richard Roundtree, and Cicely Tyson. The Agency was later renamed the Ophelia DeVore Organization, shortly after, she created a makeup line for women of color, and produced the first beauty pageant for African-American women in the United States. In her continuing mission to create a fashion-oriented culture for African-Americans, she started a fashion column that appeared in The Pittsburgh Courier, an African-American newspaper. In 1955, DeVore and her models made history once again, as she hosted ABC's weekly television show "Spotlight in Harlem." This was the first television program in New York City that was produced by, and for African-Americans. During her career, Devore served on several boards and committees under four U.S. Presidents, including the President's Advisory Committee on the Arts, she also served as an Ambassador for the Kennedy Center for Performing Arts in Washington, D.C. In 2004, she was honored by the Fashion Institute of Technology for her contributions to fashion and entertainment.

Entrepreneur and model, Ophelia DeVore is known internationally as a pioneer for her efforts in the fields of beauty, fashion, modeling, and entertainment. Growing up in Edgefield, S.C., she later moved to New York City, where she graduated from Hunter College High School and went on to attend New York University. During this time she began doing occasional modeling jobs, and later became the first African-American fashion model in the United States. Soon after, she was working exclusively for the newly formed Ebony Magazine.

In 1946, she enrolled in the Vogue School of Modeling, which until that time had excluded women of color. Later that year, DeVore along with four of her colleagues founded the Grace Del Marco Modeling Agency as a way to help create opportunities for models of color. In 1948, she created The Ophelia DeVore School of Self-Development and Modeling. She opened the doors of modeling and television in the late 1940's and early 1950's for men and women of African-American heritage and other minorities in the country.

In 1955, award winning actress, Cicely Tyson, who graced the cover of Ebony Magazine was registered with Grace Del Marco Models at the time of the publication. Throughout the 1960's, DeVore continued to revolutionize nearly every facet of the modeling and beauty industry. She created two of the first nationally known ethnic beauty contests in the U.S., developed a fashion column for the Pittsburgh Courier Newspaper and created a line of cosmetics specially formulated for people of color.

She was also a civil rights activist who received personal accolades from Dr. Martin Luther King, Jr. In addition to creating opportunities to showcase African-Americans in magazines, on the runway, in pageants and fashion shows, she produced several New York City cable television shows, including the "Ophelia DeVore Show," which to date, became one of the longest running cable shows on television. She paved the way for many modern day talk show hosts. DeVore changed the face of the beauty, fashion and entertainment industries, her business savviness was recognized all over the world, which began to spread positive news about people of color.

Through her modeling agency and school, she fostered and promoted the careers of some of the country's top African-American models, entertainers and television personalities. Through her wide and diverse involvement in nearly every facet of the modeling, beauty, fashion, entertainment, marketing and news industries, DeVore has helped society move closer to realizing her own mission. She wanted to create a movement of African-American beauty and pride.

73

John Mercer Langston

As one of the most prominent African-American political figures in the United States in the 19th century, John Mercer Langston's (1829 - 1897) advocacy for the advancement of African-Americans before and after the civil war left both a legacy and a blueprint for future civil rights leaders to follow. Langston grew up in Ohio, he served as an attorney and a clerk of Brownhelm Township, he continued to practice law in Ohio until the outbreak of the civil war. After Massachusetts Governor John Andrew began recruiting for the 54th Massachusetts Volunteer Infantry Regiment, one of the first U.S. military regiments to include African-American soldiers, Langston helped to recruit men from Ohio, Illinois, and Indiana for the Union cause. After the war, he moved to Washington D.C. in 1868 to help establish the nation's first African-American law school at (HBCU) Howard University. He became its first Dean and served briefly as acting president of Howard in 1872. In 1877, President Rutherford B. Hayes appointed Langston as Ambassador to the country of Haiti. After returning to the U.S. in 1885, he became the first President of (HBCU) Virginia State University. Langston then topped off his long political career by becoming the first African-American to represent the state of Virginia in the U.S. House of Representatives. As a member of Congress, he sat on the Education Committee. He proposed a national literacy test to vote in federal elections as an Amendment to the U.S. Constitution, which he believed could increase literacy for all citizens across the country.

Attorney, educator, activist, diplomat, and politician, John Mercer Langston is one of the first African-Americans who was elected to public office in the United States. Langston was born free on a plantation in Louisa County, VA., in 1829, where he and his family lived together until 1834. After his parents deaths, he and his siblings were sent to Ohio. Per his father's wishes, they were raised by Colonel William D. Gooch, who was a family friend.

Langston later went on to attend Oberlin College, one of the first colleges in the U.S. to admit African-American students. After completing his Undergraduate Degree, he continued his studies earning a Master's Degree in Theology. At the age of twenty-four, he became the first African-American to pass the Bar in the state of Ohio. As a lawyer, he dedicated himself to the pursuit of liberty and justice for all. He was active in the abolitionist movement and helped many enslaved people escape North along the Ohio part of the underground railroad, he also helped to recruit African-American troops during the civil war.

During his time of recruiting troops for the war, Langston along with Frederick Douglass, and other civil rights activists became the founding members of the National Equal Rights League (NERL) in 1864. NERL was one of the earliest organizations dedicated to civil rights, Langston was elected as its first president. The organization called for full and immediate citizenship for African-Americans, based on the sacrifices they made on the battlefield during the civil war.

They also believed that African-American men deserved the right to vote. After founding the national organization, state branches developed in Pennsylvania, North Carolina, Louisiana, Ohio, Missouri, Michigan, and Massachusetts. Langston advocated for the NERL's platform, bringing it specifically to several Presidents of the United States, he played an important role in shaping African-American life following the civil war. NERL remained a prominent organization until the rise of the National Association for the Advancement of Colored People (NAACP), which followed in Langston's footsteps, as well as other civil rights activists of the time.

He believed that education was essential and helped to develop one of the first law schools in the United States to admit African-Americans, Howard University School of Law. In 1888, he decided to run for Congress as a representative for Virginia. As a member of Congress, he advocated for greater protection of African-American voting rights, a national industrial university to teach African-Americans labor skills, the appointment of African-American candidates to the U.S. Military Academy at West Point, and the U.S. Naval Academy Annapolis.

Annie Turnbo Malone

Annie Turnbo Malone (1877 - 1957) founded and developed a prominent commercial and educational enterprise centered on cosmetics for African-American women. Around the turn of the 20th century, she developed a hair product to straighten African-American women's hair without causing damage, like other products available during the time. While creating an entire line of hair care and beauty products, Malone recognized she needed a larger market in which to sell her products. She moved her business to St. Louis in 1902, due to the city's economy was booming in preparation for the 1904 World's Fair. She then became a leading cosmetic entrepreneur and a leader in the St. Louis African-American community. Malone trademarked her beauty products under the name "Poro," which is a West African term that means "physical and spiritual growth." Her business grew rapidly, and she opened Poro College in 1918. The institution became the first African-American college in the country dedicated to cosmetology. Poro gave women the means and resources to change their lives. Thousands of women wanted to join the Poro team. One of her most famous students was Sarah Breedlove, who was also known as Madam C. J. Walker. She was a Poro Agent, protégé of Malone, and eventually a leading competitor of the company. By the end of World War I, Malone was a multi-millionaire, and one of the most successful and wealthiest African-American women in the country.

Entrepreneur, educator, chemist, and philanthropist, Annie Turnbo Malone is considered to be one of the first African-American women to become a self-made millionaire. Born in Metropolis, IL, to formerly enslaved parents, her father enlisted with the Union Army to assist with war efforts during the civil war. During her childhood in the late 19th century, African-American women began wearing their hair straight, at the time these methods often used unhealthy ingredients that could be dangerous to the hair and scalp.

Along with her understanding of chemistry and with the help of her aunt who was a herbal doctor, Malone created a new product which created a safer way to straighten hair. In 1902, she moved to St. Louis, taking her creation to the home of the nation's fourth largest African-American population. She was quite successful at selling her new hair product door-to-door, shortly after she trademarked her beauty products under the name "Poro." In 1918, she then opened the first U.S. Educational Institution dedicated to African-American cosmetology named Poro College.

The school served as a training center and offered African-American women a place to advance themselves. The facility housed Malone's business operation while also serving as a place for the African-American community to gather for various civic functions. The complex, which was valued at more than $1 million, included classrooms, barber shops, laboratories, auditorium, dining facilities, a theater, gymnasium, chapel, and a roof garden. Many local and national organizations, including the National Negro Business League were invited to the facility in order to use it for business functions.

More than 75,000 students graduated from Poro College, they were all trained with her new method of straightening hair, she also employed more than 175 instructors. One of her protégés was Sarah Breedlove, better known as Madam C.J. Walker, who later built her own successful empire rivaling Malone, as she also sold and distributed African-American hair products throughout the country.

In the 1920's, Malone became one of the wealthiest African-American women in the nation, with an estimated net worth of $14 million. She was a leading cosmetic entrepreneur as well as a leader in the St. Louis African-American community. She was also an active philanthropist, her generosity raised her stature in the community as she contributed thousands of dollars to educational programs, universities, the YMCA, and to nearly every African-American orphanage in the country. In 1930, Malone moved her business to Chicago, where its location became known as the Poro Block.

Loïs Mailou Jones

Loïs Mailou Jones (1905 - 1998) was a highly regarded artist and teacher whose career spanned over seven decades. Influenced by the Harlem Renaissance movement, she broadened the idea of African-American painting and scholarship. Through countless international trips and research into a variety of art forms, Jones broadened the idea of what African-American art can be. Her extensive travels throughout Europe, Africa, and the Caribbean influenced changed how she painted. Working at the Art Department at Howard University, she has trained several generations of African-American artists, including David Driskell, Elizabeth Catlett, and Sylvia Snowden, eventually becoming one of the school's most eminent professors. Throughout her career, she has championed the international artistic achievement of African-American art. Known to paint portraits and landscapes in brighter colors and intricate patterns, her paintings became bold and abstract. Her paintings have hung in the White House and are in the permanent collections of major museums around the world including the Smithsonian American Art Museum, the Metropolitan Museum of Art, and the National Museum of Women in the Arts. She was also commissioned by the United States Information Agency to serve as a Cultural Ambassador to Africa. Jones was one of the most notable figures in the world to attain fame for her art.

Highly regarded as one of the most influential artists and teachers of the 20th century, Loïs Mailou Jones forged an eclectic artistic path that had a profound influence over generations of African-American artists. Growing up in Boston, MA., she displayed an early passion for drawing. Her parents encouraged this interest by enrolling her in the High School of Practical Arts where she majored in Art. In 1927, she graduated with honors from the Boston Museum of Fine Arts and continued her education at the Designers Art School.

A year later, Jones formed and chaired the Art Department at Palmer Memorial Institute, a prep school in North Carolina. In 1928, she accepted a position at Howard University where her art courses helped shape the careers of notable artists such as Elizabeth Catlett and Starmanda Bullock. While teaching at Howard, she was awarded a General Education Board Fellowship to study at the Art School of Académie Julian in Paris. Relishing in the freedom from racial prejudice that she found in France, Jones spent many summers there.

Funded by Howard, Jones traveled to eleven African nations, she began painting portraits and landscapes in brighter colors and with a more expressionistic style. African influences began to emerge in her art, particularly after two extensive research tours of Africa. Her paintings became bold and abstract, and African design elements began to dominate, her most celebrated painting, "Les Fetiches," which was a depiction of African Masks. Upon her return to the United States, she shared the fruits of her research by organizing exhibitions, lecturing, teaching new techniques, while making the research materials she gathered available to her students and others.

Jones was one of the most notable figures in the country to attain fame for her Art, despite a prolific and lengthy career, she never had significant private gallery representation due to racial and gender discrimination. However, in 1980, President Jimmy Carter presented her with the Award for Outstanding Achievement in the Visual Arts, President Bill Clinton also hung one of her seascapes paintings in the White House while he was in office. Her paintings are in the permanent collections of more than 16 museums worldwide.

Throughout her career, Jones has championed the international artistic achievement of African-American art. Cited for her outstanding contributions as both artist and teacher, she was elected as a fellow of London's Royal Society of Arts. Her special contribution to the Black Arts Movement was her longstanding dedication to the art of classical and contemporary Africa, and its diaspora.

Dr. John Henry Hale

In 1916, accomplished surgeon, Dr. John Henry Hale (1878 - 1944) and his wife Millie Hale (1881 - 1930) converted the second floor of their home into a make-shift hospital for African-American patients who were turned away from all other hospitals in the early 1900's. Their home was located near John's alma mater, Meharry Medical College, which is a private Historically Black Medical School affiliated with the United Methodist Church in Nashville, TN. The hospital would soon take over the entire house and officially become the Millie E. Hale Infirmary in 1916. Starting as a 12-bed facility, the hospital eventually grew to include 75 beds with a laboratory, maternity ward, and operating room. More than 4,000 patients were treated at the facility, they traveled from neighboring states including Georgia, Alabama, Florida, Kentucky, North Carolina, and Texas. Millie, who was a nurse, ran the operation. As a surgeon, John conducted over 30,000 operations at the hospital, he also worked as a professor at Meharry. He conducted multiple teaching clinics all over the South to spread his surgical knowledge and practice among fellow African-American doctors. He also gave financial support to several Historically Black College and University's (HBCU's) and served as President of the National Medical Association in 1935. Hale and his wife Millie were both inducted into the Tennessee Healthcare Hall of Fame.

Surgeon, professor, and philanthropist, Dr. John Henry Hale played a critical role in establishing the African-American medical community in the early 20th century. Growing up in Estill Springs, TN., he later moved to Nashville and attended Walden University, where he graduated with a B.S. Degree in 1901. For the next four years, he attended Meharry Medical College, graduating as a Doctor of Medicine in 1905. After his graduation from Meharry, Hale was invited to join the college full-time as a faculty member and medical practitioner.

Inspired by his mentor, Daniel Hale Williams, an African-American surgeon, who in 1893 performed the first successful open heart surgery in the United States, Hale later became a prolific surgeon himself. He devoted most of his time and income to help out the African-American community in Nashville. He and his wife, Millie E. Hale contributed significantly to the health and welfare of Nashville's African-American population in the early 20th century by establishing a small hospital for those turned away by other institutions.

As a graduate of Fisk University, Millie then attended Graduate School for Nurses in New York City. Together John and Millie opened the "Millie E. Hale Hospital" on July 1, 1916, she served as its Head Nurse and Chief Administrator. The facility did not charge patients, the Hale's performed medical procedures free of charge and payed for medicines out of their own pocket. The family gradually converted their home into a hospital, community center, and meeting place of numerous organizations working to improve the lives of local people. They also distributed free food and provided home care to the poorest people in their community.

The facility grew from an original 12 beds to 75 beds, then leading to several thousand patients by 1923, eventually becoming a training center for local nurses. In addition to providing much needed medical care to the African-American community, the Millie E. Hale Hospital provided other services and conducted a variety of beneficial charitable and social programs. The facility gave instruction in health education and assisted the poor and the elderly with basic needs such as food and fuel, it also managed a prenatal and infant clinic.

Hale is credited for significant and extensive contributions to the development of African-American medicine, teaching many young physicians who all admired him. He became internationally known for his medical work. The President of his alma mater, Meharry Medical College believed that Hale had more influence than any other man in the encouragement and development of African-American surgeons worldwide.

Ella Baker

Ella Baker (1903 - 1986) was an essential activist during the civil rights movement. She began her involvement with the National Association for the Advancement of Colored People (NAACP) in 1940 working as a field secretary, then serving as director of branches from 1943 until 1946. Inspired by the historic Montgomery AL., bus boycott in 1955, Baker co-founded the organization "In Friendship" to raise money to fight against Jim Crow laws in the Deep South. In 1957, she moved to Atlanta GA., to help organize Dr. Martin Luther King Jr's new organization, the "Southern Christian Leadership Conference" (SCLC). Dr. King served as the SCLC's first president and Baker as its director. She also ran a voter registration campaign called the "Crusade for Citizenship." On February 1, 1960, a group of African-American college students from North Carolina A&T University refused to leave a Woolworth's lunch counter in Greensboro, N.C., where they had been denied service. Baker left the SCLC after the Greensboro sit-ins. She wanted to assist the students because she viewed young emerging activists as a resource and an asset to the movement. She then organized a meeting at her alma mater, Shaw University, with student leaders in April, 1960. From that meeting, the Student Nonviolent Coordinating Committee (SNCC) was born. Adopting the theory of non-violent action from Mahatma Gandhi, SNCC members joined with activists from the Congress of Racial Equality (CORE) to organize the 1961 Freedom Rides. In 1964, SNCC helped create "Freedom Summer," an effort to focus national attention on Mississippi's racism and to register African-American voters.

Community organizer, leader, and civil rights activist, Ella Baker was instrumental in using her skills and principles to establish many major civil rights organizations in the mid-20th century. Born in Norfolk, VA., she spent most of her childhood in rural North Carolina. After graduating high school, she attended Shaw University in Raleigh. Graduating from Shaw as the class valedictorian in 1927, she then decided to relocate to New York City in search of work.

Living in Harlem, Baker began joining social activist organizations. She later began working as a field secretary for the National Association for the Advancement of Colored People (NAACP). She traveled throughout the Deep South recruiting members, raising money, and spreading awareness about the importance of civil rights. The work was dangerous for a young African-American woman to undertake, but despite the challenges, she excelled and built a massive network for the NAACP.

Throughout her career, Baker spent more than half a century raising the political consciousness of African-Americans, she played a major role in three of the 20th century's most influential civil rights groups, the NAACP, the Southern Christian Leadership Conference (SCLC) and Student Non-violent Coordinating Committee (SNCC). While those groups typically had male figureheads, it was Baker who often utilized her skills, experience and contacts to plan events, establish protests and campaigns. She was largely a behind-the-scenes organizer who convinced many to join together peacefully and insist that they were deserving of basic human rights.

Baker believed that women were the backbone of the civil rights movement, their networks and knowledge were the bridges between big ideas and action plans on the ground. She also recognized that young people kept the spirit of the movement moving forward as they ushered in a new era in grassroots organizing. She especially recognized the potential of the students involved in sit-ins, and wanted to bring leaders of each movement together to meet one another and consider future collaborations.

Baker also worked alongside some of the most noted civil rights leaders of the 20th century, including W. E. B. Du Bois, Thurgood Marshall, A. Philip Randolph, and Dr. Martin Luther King Jr. She was a respected and influential leader who became one of the foremost advocates for human rights in the country. Her influence was reflected in the nickname she acquired, "Fundi," a Swahili word meaning a person who teaches a craft to the next generation. Her guidance and encouragement helped tens of thousands of activists fight for equal rights.

Lemuel Hayes

Lemuel Haynes (1753 - 1833) was a patriot involved in the American Revolutionary War, and the first African-American ordained as a Christian Minister in the United States, he was also the first African-American in the country to receive an Honorary Degree. When the United States was claiming its independence in 1776, Hayes was advocating against the colonization movement, arguing that people of African descent living in the country should be entitled to the same rights as others. In 1804, Middlebury College in Vermont awarded him a Master's Degree at its second commencement. He was an early anti-slavery advocate, who was a writer and speaker on the topic years before other famous abolitionists such as Frederick Douglass. At the age of twenty-one, he was ordained in the Congregational Church, which later became the United Church of Christ. Haynes developed an international reputation as a preacher and writer, he ministered an African-American and Caucasian congregation, which was a historical phenomenon that took place during the time. His reputation grew steadily for more than thirty years in Connecticut and Vermont, drawing people from neighboring communities and hours away. Haynes was the first African-American abolitionist to reject slavery on theological grounds. As a former indentured servant, he saw troubling inconsistencies between the Declaration of Independence claim that "All Men Are Created Equal," and the ongoing institution of slavery in America.

Clergyman, veteran, and abolitionist, Lemuel Haynes accomplished many firsts in America. As a child of racially mixed parents he was abandoned as a five month old baby. He was brought to a family by the name of Rose where he was indentured as a servant. He would gain his freedom after working for the family until 1774. The Rose family raised him as their own and he was brought up with strong gospel teaching in their home. Hayes became a follower of Jesus Christ, who would one day call him to be a preacher of the gospel in New England.

Upon gaining his freedom he volunteered to fight as a Minuteman in the militia of Massachusetts. In 1776, he joined up with the continental army in the American Revolutionary War and fought in several battles for the American colonies. During this time his views were shaped by his admiration of federalist who believed in the sharing of power among the states and the federal government. After serving in the army, he trained for gospel ministry studying the biblical languages under two Connecticut ministers.

He was licensed to preach in 1780, and five years later he became the first African-American ordained by any religious group in America. In 1788, he received a call to pastor congregations in Connecticut, Vermont, Massachusetts, and New York, where he served faithfully for over thirty years. During his time in Vermont as a paster, he received an Honorary Master's Degree from Middlebury College in 1804, which was a first for an African-American in the country.

Haynes developed a reputation for a staunch opposition to slavery and oppression, his dynamic sermons and essays which stressed liberty, natural rights, and justice were distributed in newspapers internationally, making him one of the first African-Americans to be published. He was the first African-American to publicly speak boldly and truthfully about the degradation of slavery and the contradictions of United States leaders.

In 1776, after reading the Declaration of Independence, and before his official ministry, Haynes was so inspired that he wrote his own essay, which became the first abolitionist essay ever published in the new nation of America, it was called, "Liberty Further Extended." He made the strongest argument for why the Declaration of Independence needed to specifically include enslaved people. He was the first African-American abolitionist to publicly reject slavery on purely theological grounds, rather than hiding behind social, economic, or civic arguments for the abolishment of slavery. He inspired future generations of activist as he often spoke out on important issues. Many local government leaders attended his church services in the 1790's and applauded his sermons.

Dr. Alexa Irene Canady

Dr. Alexa Irene Canady (1950 -) broke gender and color barriers by becoming the first African-American woman in the United States to become a Neurosurgeon. As a pioneer for both women physicians and African-Americans, she chose to specialize as a Pediatric Neurosurgeon for her love of children. After training at the Children's Hospital of Philadelphia, she then worked in pediatric neurosurgery at the Henry Ford Hospital in Detroit. In 1987, she became Chief of Neurosurgery at the Children's Hospital of Michigan. While earning accolades for her patient-centered approach to medicine, her department was regarded as one of the best in the country under her guidance. In addition to her other responsibilities, she conducted research and taught as a Clinical Professor of Neurosurgery at Wayne State University. Canady was also certified by the American Board of Neurological Surgery, another first for a woman. Throughout her twenty year career in pediatric neurosurgery, she has treated tens of thousands of patients, with the majority being ten years old or younger. As she spent her career breaking glass ceilings, Canady was inducted into the Michigan Women's Hall of Fame in 1989 and received the American Medical Women's Association President's Award in 1993.

Trailblazer, Dr. Alexa Irene Canady is the first African-American woman in the the country to become a Neurosurgeon as well as the first to be board certified in neurosurgery. Growing up in Lansing, MI., her parents taught her the importance of hard work and learning, which helped her to graduate from high school with honors. While attending the University of Michigan, a health career summer program for minority students sparked her interest in medicine. After graduating from college in 1971, she continued on to the university's medical school.

After attending a summer medical program for minority students, she became inspired by the magic of medicine. Initially Canady studied internal medicine, her plans then changed when she fell in love with neurosurgery. Although many advisers discouraged her from pursuing this career path, she refused to give up, as she encountered difficulties in obtaining an internship. Determined to pursue her goal of becoming a neurosurgeon, she was accepted as a surgical intern at Yale-New Haven Hospital and graduated from medical school in 1975.

When her internship ended in 1976, Canady relocated to the University of Minnesota, becoming a resident of the university's department of neurosurgery, she gained a reputation as a talented physician who loved what she did. She then chose the field of pediatric neurosurgery, her decision for this specialty was due to her love of working with children. Upon completing her residency in 1981, she then became the country's first African-American woman neurosurgeon.

While excelling in her specialty, Canady advanced in her surgical technique throughout her career. Recognized for her contributions to pediatric medicine, she was promoted countless times due to her talent and expertise. In 1984, she was certified by the American Board of Neurological Surgery, which was another first for an African-American woman. Three years later, she became the Chief of Neurosurgery at the Children's Hospital in Detroit, MI. Under her guidance, the department was soon viewed as one of the best in the country.

Canady has offered her time, service, and expertise to an extensive list of professional healthcare organizations including the American Association of Neurological Surgeons, Congress of Neurological Surgeons, and the Detroit and Medical Society. She continued to excel in learning, researching, and practicing in her field, her research ultimately led to the creation of several groundbreaking treatments for children. After retiring from Children's Hospital of Michigan, she moved to Pensacola, FL. She soon discovered the community lacked pediatric neurosurgeons. She came out of retirement and resumed her critical and life-saving work. She was also a consultant at Sacred Heart Hospital.

Thomas Mundy Peterson

In the wake of the Confederate States being defeated by the United States of America during the civil war, the 13th, 14th, and 15th Amendments to the Constitution were instituted. Thomas Mundy Peterson (1824 - 1904) then became the first African-American in the United States to exercise his right to vote and cast his ballot in a New Jersey election. He cast his historic vote on March 31, 1870. The iconic vote was in a local election in Perth Amboy, N.J. for the town's charter. Passed by Congress on February 26, 1869, and ratified February 3, 1870, the 15th Amendment granted African-American men the right to vote. The citizens of Perth Amboy, N.J. later awarded Peterson a medallion in 1884 which displayed the face of Abraham Lincoln engraved on one side, and the opposite side read "presented by the citizens of Perth Amboy to Thomas Peterson." The 13th Amendment abolished slavery in America, while the 14th Amendment granted citizenship to all persons born in the United States, including formerly enslaved people, and provided them with equal protection under the laws. After the civil war ended, the 15th Amendment granted citizens the right to vote regardless of race, color, or previous servitude. Peterson's participation in the election symbolized the beginning of voting rights for all people in America. He remained active in Perth Amboy's politics, continuing to vote each year and even serving on the towns committee to revise the city's charter. Through his actions, he joined the many New Jersey citizens who has pushed forward the cause of liberty.

Community leader and resident of Perth Amboy N.J., Thomas Mundy Peterson is the first African-American to vote in a United States election after the passage of the 15th Amendment of the Constitution granted all men the right to vote. The passage of the 15th Amendment in 1870 ignited the African-American community and kicked off extensive celebrations across the country, many calling the historical moment, "The Nation's Second Birth" and a "Greater Revolution than that of 1776." It is recorded that several thousand African-American men and women marched down Broadway in New York City cheering the victory.

Following the approval of the 15th Amendment, African-Americans, many of whom were formerly enslaved, utilized their newly won freedom to vote by electing a new wave of first time African-American candidates. In the decade of reconstruction that followed, twenty-two African-American representatives were voted in as members of congress. Within the first month, on March 31, 1870, the first vote was cast in Perth Amboy, N.J. by Peterson. His historic vote came in a city that had once been a major stop along the underground railroad. As the son of a formally enslaved parent, Peterson was born in Metuchen, N.J. in 1824.

By 1828, his family moved to Perth Amboy, New Jersey which had become an enclave of progressive idealists. He grew up and began work as a handyman and janitor at local School No. 1. (That same school was named after him in 1989). At the age of thirty-four, he attended Perth Amboy's local election casting his ballot in favor of revising an existing city charter, making him the first African-American to vote in any election in United States history. This event helped to set the precedent by which the turning away of African-Americans from the ballot box could no longer be legally or constitutionally supported.

As a registered voter, Peterson also became the first African-American person in Perth Amboy to serve on a jury, he later earned the distinction of being jointly appointed to make amendments to the very charter's revisions he voted in favor of previously. Perth Amboy later celebrated the honor of Peterson's triumphant moment in American history by bestowing on him a gold medallion.

He wore his medal proudly each week to services at Perth Amboy's St. Peter's Episcopal Church. Peterson would then go on to embrace civic life, serving on juries, running for local office, and representing his hometown at political conventions. His place in history has been recognized both by the city of Perth Amboy and the State of New Jersey. In 1998, the State Legislature passed a resolution that each year March 31, be known as "Thomas Mundy Peterson Day."

Margaret Bailey

Margaret Bailey (1915 - 2014) set several landmarks for African-American nurses in the United States Military. In 1964, she became the first African-American Lieutenant-Colonel, she then advanced to Colonel in 1967, which was the highest achievable military rank in the Army Nurse Corps. She served in the Corps for twenty-seven years, spending many years in a post-war France, Germany, and Japan. While stationed abroad, Bailey frequently encountered people who had never worked with or even seen an African-American woman before. She enjoyed taking extra steps to educate others about African-American history and culture, believing these actions to be important steps towards integration. During her military career, she actively worked with minority organizations to increase African-American participation in the Corps, she also advocated for the integration of the army for all military housing, recreational facilities and working environments. After her retirement from the army, she served as a consultant to the Surgeon General in the Nixon Administration, working to increase the number of minorities in the Nurse Corps. Her efforts were commended by the National Association for the Advancement of Colored People (NAACP), which witnessed the appointment of hundreds of African-American public servants to governmental positions. Throughout her career, Bailey received several awards and commendations both for her military service and her activism.

United States Army nurse and activist, Margaret Bailey was one of the most influential African-American military nurses in U.S. history. Growing up in Selma, AL., she attended Dunbar High School. While walking past the local hospital on her way to school each day, she was intrigued and fascinated by the medical professionals she noticed, which inspired her to become a nurse early on. After graduation, she worked to save enough money to further her education. In 1935, she was accepted to the Fraternal Hospital School of Nursing in Montgomery, AL.

In 1939, Bailey decided to relocate North and accept a nursing position at Seaview Hospital in Staten Island, N.Y. During the time, this facility was the largest in the nation and the most expensive municipal medical establishment in the United States. After five years of service, she decided to enlist in the U.S. military and joined the United States Army Nurse Corps in 1944. During the time, the U.S. military was segregated. African-American women were beginning to be accepted due to the pressure from the National Association of Colored Graduate Nurses and First Lady Eleanor Roosevelt.

In the mid-1940's, there were only 183 African-American nurses who served in an Army Corps of 52,000 nurses. During World War II, Bailey served as both a medical and surgical nurse at numerous domestic and international facilities, which were located in France, Germany, and Japan, she also treated German prisoners of war. Despite the racial discrimination she encountered, she found the war as an opportunity to fight for her citizenship, democracy, and pride.

Bailey gradually advanced through the ranks as she was promoted to Captain in 1950. After twenty years of service, she was then promoted to Lieutenant-Colonel in 1964, becoming the first African-American nurse to achieve that rank. While serving as Chief Nurse in a non-segregated unit in 1966, her career then advanced to the highest military rank possible within the United States Army Nurse Corps, in which she became the first African-American Colonel.

Bailey set many standards for African-American military nurses during her career, she shattered multiple glass ceilings while actively working with minority organizations, and advocated to increase African-American participation in the Corps. After her retirement from the army in 1971, she accepted a position of Consultant to the Surgeon General of the United States. Bailey also became an activist who was in contact with several women's rights organizations who promoted an increased participation of minorities in the Army Nurse Corps. She increased her efforts by regularly giving speeches in communities across the country to promote integration and military service.

William "Bill" Pickett

Rodeo Cowboy, William Pickett, (1870 - 1932) also known as Bill Pickett, was one of the first great rodeo cowboys and is credited with inventing the sport and technique of "Bulldogging," the skill of grabbing cattle by the horns and wrestling them to the ground. Pickett entered his first rodeo in 1888 at a fair in Taylor, TX. By the early 1900's he became a popular rodeo performer. During his career, he was often known by the nicknames "The Dusky Demon" and "The Bull-Dogger," and was billed as "The World Champion in death-defying feats of courage and skill." He also performed in a number of motion pictures and is credited with being the first African-American Cowboy Star. In 1971, he became the first African-American inducted into the National Cowboy Hall of Fame, and in 1989 was also honored in the Pro Rodeo Hall of Fame. His image decorates one of the most famous, and collectible, postage stamps ever issued by the U.S. Postal Service. To honor his legacy, The Bill Pickett Invitational Rodeo, which is the longest running African-American rodeo in the U.S. was founded in 1984 by Lu Vason. The Invitational Rodeo brings the history of African-American Cowboys to the forefront, as well as develop the next generation of rodeo stars, the event also brings the sport of rodeo to a new generation of fans.

Rodeo Cowboy, wild west show performer, and actor, Bill Pickett was the originator of rodeo steer wrestling, or bulldogging. Growing up in Travis County, TX., in the 1870's, his parents were of African-American and Native-American descent. He attended school through the 5th grade and then began to work at ranching. By the time he was eighteen, his family had moved to Taylor, TX., where he and his brothers began a horse-breaking and cowboy service called "Pickett Brothers Bronco Busters and Rough Riders Association."

In 1907, Pickett signed with the 101 Ranch Wild West Show, becoming one of its star performers and assuming the status of a legendary figure for his masterful handling of both wild and domestic animals. Credited with inventing the technique of "steer wrestling," or "bulldogging," he perfected a technique of jumping from his horse, grabbing the steer around the neck or horns, and pulling it to the ground. The show toured around the country and even appeared in early motion pictures. Pickett's widely popular performances imbedded the image of an African-American cowboy to tens of thousands of fans nationwide.

His image as a skilled, charismatic, crowd-pleasing cowboy set the standard which influenced all of his successors and helped mass audiences redefine what African-American men had accomplished in the American West. The more he toured the country performing his bulldogging act, the name Bill Pickett soon became synonymous with successful rodeos.

In 1977, world renown music and show promoter, Lu Vason noticed an absence of African-American cowboys and cowgirls participating in national rodeos. As a leader in the entertainment industry, he was motivated by a desire to give them a platform to showcase their talents. He understood the rich history of the rodeo and its importance to the community, and to keep Pickett's legacy alive. In 1984, he created The Bill Picket Invitational Rodeo (BPIR), serving as both as an entertainment and educational event which highlights the contributions of African-American cowboys and cowgirls. Vason wanted to make sure that fans attending his rodeo knew the importance of Pickett and the history of the rodeo.

His invitational rodeo is America's only touring African-American rodeo which travels to more than 30 cities across the country, attracting more than 130,000 fans annually. Pickett became the most famous African-American cowboy entertainer in American history. In 1987, the North Fort Worth Historical Society commissioned a bronze statue showing Pickett bulldogging a one-thousand pound longhorn. The lifelike sculpture sits on the grounds of Fort Worth's Cowtown Coliseum where he performed during its grand opening in 1908.

93

Dr. Rebecca Lee Crumpler

In 1864, a thirty-three year old woman named Rebecca Lee Crumpler (1831 - 1895) became the first African-American woman in the United States to earn a Medical Degree. Her Degree in Medicine was awarded by the New England Female Medical College, a pioneering institution that merged a decade later with Boston University and formed Boston University School of Medicine (BUSM). Following her graduation, Crumpler continued to be a pioneer in the field of medicine by working for the newly formed Freedmen's Bureau in Richmond, VA. The Bureau was created at the end of the civil war to serve recently freed enslaved people and help them gain access to food, housing, and medical services. Recognizing their was a greater need than what the Bureau could serve, she moved back to Boston and published, "A Book of Medical Discourses," one of the earliest medical publications by an African-American physician. Her book focused on preventing disease, just as much as on curing them, It also chronicled her experiences as a doctor and provides guidance on maternal and child health. She wrote using as few technical terms as possible, it did not divide health along racial lines, it simply provided the best medical practices for the benefit of all people alike. Her legacy is honored each year on her birthday, February 8th, it was officially established as "National Black Women Physicians Day." The day was recognized with a proclamation by Congress, as Crumpler has inspired generations of African-American women in the field of healthcare.

Physician, nurse, and author, Dr. Rebecca Lee Crumpler was a trailblazer and dreamer who believed she could make a difference in the world. Born Rebecca Davis in Delaware in 1831, Crumpler was raised by an aunt in Pennsylvania who often helped care for their sick neighbors. Those early experiences made her want to work to "relieve the suffering of others." In the early 1850's she moved to Massachusetts and became a nurse.

In 1860, Crumpler became the first, and only African-American woman accepted to the New England Female Medical College (NEFMC). This was the first women's medical college globally to train women medical doctors during the time. The NEFMC initially trained women to work only as midwives, by the time Crumpler attended, the curriculum expanded to encompass a more complete medical education. She graduated in 1864, becoming the first African-American woman Doctor in the U.S., her official Degree was "Doctress of Medicine."

She began practicing in Boston, but at the end of the civil war she found herself drawn to Richmond, VA. to volunteer her services as a physician. The war had stretched the medical system to its limit, countless veterans and civilians needed extreme medical care, creating more opportunities for non-traditional medical students. Crumpler collaborated with the Freedmen's Bureau along with other missionary groups to care for formerly enslaved men, women, and children.

The majority of her patients had no access to medical care beyond what the Freedmen's Bureau and volunteers were willing to provide due to poverty and lack of resources. The enormous needs of these patients, and the discrimination they faced from many Southern doctors, encouraged an increasing number of African-Americans to seek medical training.

Crumpler returned home to Boston in the late 1860's where she continued practicing medicine and provided medical care to women and children, she treated her patients regardless of their ability to pay. After twenty years of practicing medicine she published a medical guide book in 1883 based on clinical notes she kept during her years of practice.

Her publication, "A Book of Medical Discourses" is the first medical text written by an African-American author. The groundbreaking book covered topics not often examined in depth at the time, it chronicled her experiences as a doctor and provided guidance on maternal and child health. Along with her pioneering achievements and historical legacy as a physician, her talent and determination to help others, established health equality and social justice for generations.

Major Robert Lawrence

In 1967, Major Robert Lawrence (1935 - 1967) was the first African-American to be selected as an astronaut by any national space program. As a highly accomplished U.S. Air Force (USAF) Fighter Pilot with a Doctorate in Physical Chemistry, he was selected to train for a highly secretive mission to spy on the Soviet Union from space. Lawrence was selected to become part of a classified military space program called the Manned Orbiting Laboratory (MOL) program the day after he graduated from the U.S. Air Force Test Pilot school. Publicly, the goal of the joint Air Force and National Reconnaissance Office project was to study whether crewed spaceflight could be useful for the military. Behind the scenes, however, MOL's real goal was to keep an eye on the Soviet Union from low polar orbit. From a series of small orbiting stations, two-man crews composed entirely of Air Force Officers, spent 30 days at a time photographing Soviet operations around the world. The MOL program was a joint project of the U.S. Air Force and the National Reconnaissance Office to obtain high-resolution photographic imagery of America's Cold War adversaries. Being in polar orbit had an advantage of the Earth rotating beneath the orbital path, giving satellites a chance to view the entire planet once a day. Due to the secrecy surrounding the MOL program, Lawrence's name remained largely unknown for years. He later received the proper recognition for his service and accomplishments.

United States Air Force Officer Major Robert Lawrence was the first African-American selected as an astronaut by a national space program. Growing up in Chicago IL., he graduated from high school at the age of sixteen. After earning his Bachelor's Degree in Chemistry from Bradley University at the age of twenty, he became a U.S. Air Force (USAF) officer and pilot. Lawrence was a highly accomplished pilot with over 2,500 flying hours, he later earned a PhD in Physical Chemistry from Ohio State University in 1965. His flight hours provided the experience needed to achieve what few others could, to be an astronaut.

Although many talented pilots such as Lawrence submitted applications to NASA's space program, there was an alternative in 1967. The USAF had a space program of its own, a vision of militarized space exploration promoted by NASA. Lawrence was selected as a member of a group of aerospace research pilots for the Manned Orbiting Laboratory (MOL) program, making him the first African-American astronaut.

MOL was a top-secret joint effort between the U.S. Air Force and the National Reconnaissance Office. The USAF devised a plan to continuously place military personnel into space with a surveillance platform and capture high resolution images by crewed mini space stations in Earth's orbit. The USAF envisioned the MOL as a small space station in polar orbit, crewed by two USAF astronauts who would remain on the MOL platform for approximately 30-day missions, equipped with the Dorian Imagery System (a six-foot-diameter spy camera, which could capture items as small as a baseball looking down from space), a much higher resolution than previous systems on unmanned satellites.

Using the advanced imagery equipment, the MOL astronauts would photograph targets of military intelligence interest on Earth daily. As a senior pilot, Lawrence spent much of his career with the Air Force training other pilots in cutting edge flight maneuvers and techniques, it was during one such training session that Lawrence met his untimely death just six months after being selected for the MOL program. While practicing landing techniques later used in the space shuttle program, he perished in a crash of an F-104 Starfighter supersonic jet at Edwards Air Force Base in California.

Lawrence made the ultimate sacrifice in service to the space program, but his legacy lived on through several of his fellow MOL astronauts who joined NASA and flew space shuttle missions with the program. Although his career was cut short, he paved the way for future generations of aerospace pioneers of all races highlighting the need for diversity and inclusion across the industry.

Louis Lorenzo Redding

Along with being the first African-American Attorney in the state of Delaware and being a champion for equality, Louis Lorenzo Redding (1901 - 1998) seized the opportunity to change the legal principles that embraced racial segregation in his state and beyond. Through his efforts, in 1950 the University of Delaware broke down its racial barriers and admitted African-American students for the first time. Two years later he was successful in bringing a case to desegregate all public schools in the state of Delaware. The case had national significance, it became a part of Brown vs. Board of Education, which in 1954 resulted in the U.S. Supreme Court's declaration that the "separate but equal" doctrine was unconstitutional. Redding also fought for passage of open legislation in Delaware. During his professional life he joined the National Bar Association, the National Lawyers Guild, and the National Association for the Advancement of Colored People (NAACP), he also became President of the Delaware Bar Association. For most of his career he was legal counsel for the Wilmington NAACP. Redding spent his entire adult life fighting for the rights of African-Americans, particularly in Delaware. As an attorney, he never lost a desegregation case during his professional career.

Civil rights advocate and prominent attorney, Louis Lorenzo Redding was the first African-American man admitted to practice law in the state of Delaware. Growing up in Alexandria, VA., his parents, both from well educated upper-class families moved to Delaware from Washington, D.C., where his father taught English at Howard University. Redding attended Howard High School where one of his teachers was poet, journalist and political activist, Alice Dunbar-Nelson. He then attended Brown University, where he was the commencement speaker for his graduating class in 1923.

After graduation, Redding earned money for law school by working as an Assistant Principal at Fessenden Academy in Ocala, FL. He then taught English at Morehouse College for one year. He went on to become the only African-American graduate in the Harvard Law School Class of 1928. He returned to Wilmington where he became Delaware's first African-American lawyer. Beginning in 1929, and for the following twenty-six years, Redding remained the state's only African-American lawyer.

In 1950, Redding won a lawsuit that he brought against the University of Delaware, which barred African-American students from admission, citing the "separate but equal" doctrine. Judge Collins J. Seitz ordered the University of Delaware to began admitting African-American students. The integration of the university then led to the integration of several other locations in Delaware, including movie theaters, hospitals, restaurants, and retail stores.

In 1951, Redding undertook several other cases to desegregate public high schools in the state. These cases were combined with three other states and the District of Columbia to become part of the landmark U.S. Supreme Court case in 1954 known as Brown vs. Board of Education. Alongside a team of attorneys, which included future Supreme Court Justice Thurgood Marshall. Redding played a pivotal role and argued during the Brown case, which later unanimously declared segregation in public schools as unconstitutional.

Successfully representing victims of racial discrimination in a series of landmark cases, Redding gave new meaning to the concept of equality under the law. He practiced law for fifty-seven years, opening doors to education and accommodations for many in Delaware as well as the nation. Known for his work challenging the many segregation laws in the state, the University of Delaware honored him by naming a dormitory after him. The Redding Middle School in Middletown, DE., was also named in his honor. As an advocate for equality, he later became President of the Delaware Bar Association.

Andrew Jackson Smith

Known for his military service and heroism as a Union Soldier on the battlefield during the civil war, Corporal Andrew Jackson Smith (1843 - 1932) earned America's highest military decoration, the Congressional Medal of Honor for his actions at the Battle of Honey Hill, South Carolina. Formally enslaved, Smith learned about President Abraham Lincoln's Emancipation Proclamation, he then enlisted in the 55th Massachusetts Infantry, which was largely recruited by free African-American men across the North. Held by the Confederate Army, Honey Hill protected the railroad lines between Charleston, SC. and Savannah, GA. On November 30th, 1864, the 55th infantry fought heroically, during the battle, the enemy targeted and hit the regiment's color flag bearer and wounded the other, Smith retrieved and saved both flags and carried them through battle. (A regiment's flag was considered its heart and soul, if it was to fall on the ground or be captured by enemy forces, it was considered both failure and dishonor). Smith viewed the flag as a symbol of freedom and democracy, not only did he save the colors, but he broke through the line in a fierce battle maintaining the infantry's fighting integrity. As for the nearly 180,000 African-American soldiers who fought for the Union during the civil war, the ultimate reward was their freedom. Five months later, the war ended, the Confederate Army surrendered to the Union. Of the 1,523 medal of honor recipients during the civil war, only 26 medals were awarded to African-American troops. After the war, Smith was promoted to Sergeant.

Union Soldier and war hero, Corporal Andrew Jackson Smith was one of a few African-American civil war veterans awarded the Congressional Medal of Honor. Born enslaved in Grand Rivers, KY., he escaped at the age of nineteen and presented himself to the 41st Illinois Volunteer Infantry Regiment of the Union Army in Smithland, KY. He initially served and fought in the Battle of Shiloh which took place in Tennessee.

After being wounded, he recuperated in Clinton, IL., where he found out about the enactment of the Emancipation Proclamation, which opened the way for the enlistment of free men of color and formally enslaved men to fight for their freedom within the Union Army. Smith enlisted in the 55th Massachusetts Infantry, a volunteer regiment of soldiers mostly recruited by abolitionists such as Frederick Douglass. His regiment fought in battles along the East Coast, including the Battle of Honey Hill in South Carolina.

During this battle, Confederate troops killed one color bearer and wounded the other, Smith grabbed both flags and succeeded in maintaining the regiment's communications throughout the entire battle. Being a color bearer (soldier who carried the flag for their army) was a prestigious and important role, it made them the number one target on the field for all of the enemy soldiers. Although half of the officers and one-third of the enlisted men were killed or wounded in his infantry, Smith continued to expose himself to enemy fire by carrying the flags throughout the battle. Through his actions, the flags were not lost to the enemy.

Due to his extraordinary bravery in the face of deadly enemy fire, he continued to fight as he kept up with the highest traditions of military service. Smith was promoted to Sergeant before leaving the army in 1865, shortly after, he moved back to Kentucky and purchased land in the city of Eddyville. He was originally nominated for the medal of honor in 1916 by his regiment's surgeon, Dr. Burton Wilder, but due to inaccuracies and the omission of his actions in the battle's official report, his efforts were turned down by the war department.

Although Smith passed away in 1932, his family continued the fight to uncover the evidence necessary to prove his heroism. Two generations later, they finally discovered the proof they were looking for, first hand accounts from the Library of Congress detailed the battle and role that Smith played in saving his units flags. In 2001, President Bill Clinton signed legislation to award Smith the Medal of Honor posthumously. A ceremony was given at the White House, and the medal was received by his family, including his ninety-three year old daughter Caruth Smith Washington, who later unveiled his portrait at the Pentagon Hall of Heroes.

Frances Ellen Watson Harper

As a poet, author, and lecturer, Frances Ellen Watson Harper (1825 - 1911) was a household name in the 19th century. Not only was she the first African-American woman to publish a short story, but she was also an influential abolitionist, suffragist, and reformer that co-founded the "National Association of Colored Women's Clubs." Harper prevailed in her literature and soon began lecturing independently for abolitionism, which included readings of the many poems and essays that she had prepared over the years. She was recognized by her abolitionist peers as a "valuable acquisition to the cause" and was appointed to the position of Permanent Lecturer with the Anti-Slavery Society. She commanded large audiences with her anti-slavery lectures and poetry as she traveled across the United States and Canada. In 1854, she published Poems of Miscellaneous Subjects, which featured one of her most famous works, "Bury Me in a Free Land." She became an in-demand lecturer on behalf of the abolitionist movement, appearing with the likes of Frederick Douglass, William Garrison, Lucretia Mott, and Lucy Stone.

Abolitionist, suffragist, poet, teacher, and public speaker, Frances Ellen Watson Harper was one of the most influential women of the 19th century. Born in Baltimore, MD., in 1825 to parents who were free from slavery, she was an only child. By the time she was three years old, both of her parents passed away and she became an orphan. Harper's aunt and uncle, Henrietta and William Watkins, adopted and raised her after her parent's death. Her uncle was an outspoken abolitionist, practiced self-taught medicine, and established his own school in 1820 called the Watkins Academy for Negro Youth.

Harper learned from her uncle's activism and she attended the Watkins Academy until she was thirteen years old. At that age, children were typically expected to join the workforce. Harper took a job as a nursemaid and seamstress for a Quaker family that owned a bookshop. Her love for books blossomed as she spent any free time she had in the shop. By age twenty-one, Harper wrote her first small volume of poetry called "Forest Leaves."

When she was twenty-six years old, Harper left Maryland and became the first woman instructor at Union Seminary, a school for free African-Americans in Wilberforce, OH. She taught domestic science for a year and then moved to a school in York, Pennsylvania. Shortly after she began working as a teacher, her home state of Maryland passed a law stating that free African-Americans living in the North were no longer allowed to enter the state of Maryland, if found, they would be imprisoned or enslaved. Harper was now unable to return to her own home. She decided to devote all of her efforts to the anti-slavery cause.

She began writing poetry for anti-slavery newspapers, her poem "Eliza Harris," was published in "The Liberator," and in Frederick Douglass newspaper, "The North Star." By the time Harper left Philadelphia in 1854, she had compiled her second small volume of poetry called "Poems on Miscellaneous Subjects" with an introduction by abolitionist William Lloyd Garrison, she also traveled across the United States and Canada as a lecturer.

In addition to her anti-slavery lectures, Harper was committed to the struggle for women's rights, she included her observations from her travels in her writings and began to publish novels, short stories, and poetry focused on issues of racism, feminism and classism. In 1866, she spoke at the National Woman's Rights Convention in New York. Her famous speech "We Are All Bound Up Together," urged attendees to include African-American women in their fight for suffrage. The next day, a meeting was held to organize the "Equal Rights Association" to began work for the rights of both African-Americans and women.

John Harold Johnson

Widely regarded as the most influential African-American publisher in
American history, John H. Johnson (1918 - 2005) was a cultural icon who
forever changed the world of publishing and entertainment. He founded
Ebony Magazine in 1945, and Jet Magazine in 1951. Both publications
provided a much needed national forum to millions of African-Americans,
its content centered on entertainment, business, health, politics, sports,
fashion, and beauty tips. The influence of the magazines was immediate,
their widespread articles covered and highlighted accomplishments of
African-Americans and earned a strong reputation for its celebration
of history and culture. The magazines also covered several historical
events in the civil rights movement, including The March on Washington.
In 1971, he created Johnson Publishing Company to oversee his
publications in Chicago, IL. His company then diversified and expanded
into book publishing, several radio stations, insurance, and cosmetics
manufacturing. He later initiated Fashion Fair Cosmetics, the largest
African-American-owned cosmetics company in the world. Johnson,
who was named to the Forbes list of 400 richest Americans, served on the
board of directors of several Fortune 500 corporations. He also served as
a special United States Ambassador for Presidents John F. Kennedy and
Lyndon B. Johnson. In 1996, on the 50th anniversary of Ebony magazine,
he received the Presidential Medal of Freedom from President Bill Clinton.

Entrepreneur, visionary, and philanthropist, John Harold Johnson built a publishing empire that helped to forever change the perception of African-Americans in the United States. Growing up in rural Arkansas City, AR., during the 1920's, his family later relocated North to Chicago, IL., in search for greater opportunities. While attending DuSable High School, some of his famous classmates included singer, Nat King Cole and comedian, Redd Foxx. He secured a scholarship to attend the University of Chicago after his 1936 graduation.

As a student, Johnson worked part time at the Supreme Liberty Life Insurance Company. He rose to the position of editor of the company's monthly newspaper and quickly saw a need and opportunity for a magazine targeting African-American audiences. He crafted an innovative idea of asking all of Supreme Life's members via its mailing list to buy into the new digest he wanted to create, which would be known as "The Negro Digest."

In 1942, he mailed the first issue of Negro Digest, which became an instant hit and led to the creation of two other magazines, Ebony and Jet, which were initiated in 1945 and 1951, shortly after, he began Johnson Publishing Company. Ebony went on to become the No. 1 African-American magazine in the world, with three-million monthly readers. Jet also became the No. 1 newsweekly magazine, with more than nine-million subscribers. Both publications provided visual commentary on African-American life, filling a much-needed void in the American publishing sector. His magazines were also at the forefront of the civil rights movement, its articles reported on several pieces of landmark legislations.

Johnson was also instrumental in persuading corporate America to advertise in his publications and depict people of color in those advertisements. He was a gifted businessman and leader who gave a voice to millions of African-Americans with positive images and stories through print. His multi-million dollar empire eventually combined publishing, cosmetics, and insurance. In 1958, he initiated the hugely successful Ebony Fashion Fair, the world's largest traveling fashion show, which has raised over $50 million for charity since its inception.

Although the Johnson's Publishing Company was a diversified powerhouse, Ebony and Jet remained the pillars of its prosperity. In 1982, he became the first African-American named to the Forbes list of the 400 richest Americans. Johnson was without question the most important force in African-American publishing in the 20th century, and has been credited with single-handedly opening the commercial magazine marketplace to people of color worldwide.

Dr. Dorothy Lavinia Brown

Dr. Dorothy Lavinia Brown (1919 - 2004) was the first African-American woman Surgeon in the South. After receiving her Bachelor's Degree, she went on to pursue her Medical Degree at Meharry Medical College in Nashville, TN. She interned for one year at Harlem Hospital in New York City, then chose surgery as her residency specialty. In 1955, Brown was inducted as a Fellow of the American College of Surgeons, becoming one of the few African-American women to do so. From 1957 until 1983, she was Chief of Surgery at Nashville's Riverside Hospital and was the Educational Director for the Riverside Meharry Clinical Rotation Program. She rose through the ranks at Meharry to eventually become a Clinical Professor and attending Surgeon at Hubbard Hospital. In 1970, the Dorothy L. Brown Women's Residence at Meharry Medical College was named in her honor, she also received a humanitarian award from the Carnegie Foundation for her work on behalf of women, children, and healthcare. Later in her career she entered politics, becoming the first African-American to serve in the Tennessee General Assembly as she was elected to the Tennessee House of Representatives. Brown was very active in changing laws, beginning in 1956, when an unmarried patient asked her to adopt her newborn daughter, Brown agreed and fought to become the first single adoptive parent in the state of Tennessee.

Surgeon, legislator, and educator, Dr. Dorothy Lavinia Brown was a medical pioneer and community leader known for a series of firsts. She was a trailblazer in surgery and beyond as the first African-American woman surgeon in the South. Born in Philadelphia, PA., in 1919, Brown spent her youth at a New York City orphanage. By the time she was in high school, teachers began recognizing her talents, and she was placed with a loving foster family who supported her education. After graduating at the top of her class, she wanted to fulfill her life's dream of becoming a doctor.

Brown began her career as a doctor in World War II assisting soldiers, she faced many barriers during her journey due to her race and gender. After the war, she entered medical school at Meharry Medical College inille TN., receiving her Medical Degree in 1948. After completing a year-long internship at Harlem Hospital in New York City, the next decision was her choice of residency. She returned to Meharry's George Hubbard Hospital in 1949 to complete a five-year residency. Once she completed her residency, she became an Assistant Professor of Surgery in 1955.

In 1956, Brown agreed to adopt a child from an unmarried patient at the hospital. The patient came to Brown while still pregnant and asked her to adopt her child. Brown agreed because she wanted a child and knew that a chance like this would most likely never come again. Brown became the first known single female in the state of Tennessee to legally adopt a child.

In 1966, redistricting in the state offered the successful doctor and community leader yet another challenge, a seat in the Tennessee House of Representatives was open. She won the election, becoming the first African-American woman elected to the Tennessee General Assembly. Concerned with the issues of health, education, and welfare reform, she became a champion for children, civil rights, and woman's reproductive rights.

During her career as a politician, Brown also became involved in the passing of the Negro History Act, which required public schools in Tennessee to conduct special programs during Black History Month to recognize accomplishments made by African-Americans throughout history. After serving her community as a politician, she eventually returned to full-time medical practice and remained active in the civil rights movement. Brown served as Nashville's Riverside Hospital Chief of Surgery and as Meharry's Clinical Professor of Surgery from 1959 until 1983. She went on to receive several honors, awards, accolades, and honorary degrees following her career.

Paul Robeson

Paul Robeson (1898 - 1976) was a one of the most gifted men in the history of the world. He was an athlete, actor, author, attorney, scholar, and concert singer. Recognized as an international recording artist, he performed on concert stages throughout the world. Known as the man of many talents, he was one of the top performers of his time. His travels opened his awareness to human suffering and oppression. He began to use his voice to speak out for independence, freedom, and equality for all people. He believed that artists should use their talents and exposure to aid causes around the world. Robeson spoke and performed in over twenty languages and dialects, and became a spokesman throughout the world against exploitation and injustice. Throughout his lifetime he fought against all forms of racism and oppression aimed towards African-Americans in the United States. His talents made him a revered man of his time, but his attacks on injustice and racism in the U.S. became a severe international embarrassment to the U.S. Government. Despite his contributions as an entertainer to the Allied forces during World War II, he was singled out as a major threat. Every attempt was made to silence and discredit him. In 1950, the persecution reached a climax when his passport was revoked by the U.S. State Department. As Robeson always stuck to his principles and spoke up for equality, the U.S. Supreme Court agreed with him in 1958, ruling that the State Department could not deny citizens the right to travel because of their political beliefs or affiliations.

Athlete, actor, singer, scholar, author, and political activist, Paul Robeson was the epitome of the 20th century renaissance man. Growing up in Princeton, NJ., he earned a four-year scholarship to Rutgers University, making him the third African-American to attend the school. He participated in four varsity sports (baseball, football, basketball, and track), won speech and debate tournaments, while also managing to graduate valedictorian of his class. After graduation, Robeson applied his athletic abilities to a short career in professional football.

Aside from his action on the field, he earned a Law Degree and changed the direction of his career. His legal career was cut short however due to racial discrimination during the early 1920's. He left law and turned to his childhood love of acting and singing. Robeson starred in several musicals on Broadway as well as Hollywood motion pictures, he was one of the top performers of his time. He spoke and performed in over twenty languages and became a spokesman throughout the world against exploitation, injustice, and racism.

While his fame grew in the United States, he became equally well-loved internationally. As a singer, his concert career spanned the globe in the 1930's, he toured Austria, Germany, France, Netherlands, England, Russia and the Czech Republic. His mindset changed after visiting other countries and returning home to the United States. He spoke in support of workers and common people both in other countries and in the U.S., and marched against discrimination. More than any other performer of his time, he believed that the famous have a responsibility to fight for justice and peace.

In a time of deeply entrenched racism, he continually struggled for further understanding of cultural differences. During the height of his popularity, he became a national symbol as well as a cultural leader in the war against fascism abroad and racism at home. He was admired and befriended by both the general public and prominent personalities, including First Lady Eleanor Roosevelt, W.E.B. Du Bois, Joe Louis, Lena Horne, and President Harry S. Truman. While his varied talents and outspoken defense of civil liberties brought him many admirers, it also made him enemies among conservatives trying to maintain the status quo in America.

Increasingly politically minded, Robeson eventually left his film career behind, using his international celebrity to speak for those denied their civil liberties around the world, and ultimately becoming a victim of ideological persecution himself. But his legacy lives on and continues to speak eloquently of the long and difficult journey of a courageous and outspoken African-American hero.

Ann Cole Lowe

Ann Cole Lowe (1898 - 1981) was the first renowned African-American noted Fashion Designer in the United States. Her one-of-a-kind designs were a favorite among high society matrons from the 1920's to the 1960's. By the early 1950's, with the opening of her own store on Madison Avenue in New York City, she began to dress the notable names of the Upper East Side. Her designs, which were made from the finest fabrics was an immediate success and attracted many wealthy, high society clients. While her designs regularly appeared in the pages of Vogue, Vanity Fair, and Town & Country magazines, they were also featured in department stores such as Neiman Marcus and Saks Fifth Avenue. Lowe was known for being highly selective in choosing her clientele. She created designs for several generations of the wealthiest families in the world including the Rockefeller's and the DuPont's. In 1953, she was hired to design a wedding dress for future First Lady Jacqueline Bouvier and the dresses for her bridal attendants for her wedding to then-Senator John F. Kennedy. A collection of her designs and dresses are also held at several museums across the country including New York's Metropolitan Museum of Art and the Smithsonian National Museum of African-American History and Culture in Washington D.C.

Considered one of the most significant designers in U.S. history, Ann Cole Lowe earned a reputation as the first African-American fashion designer to receive international acclaim, her designs were favored amongst many high society women for close to half a century. Growing up in Montgomery AL., she was a third generation dressmaker, her mother and grandmother were expert seamstresses. Learning from both women, Lowe became skilled at creating intricate fabrics and flower embroidering, which would later become one of her signatures pieces.

While reading a fashion magazine, Lowe, who was eager to enhance her skills, learned about the S.T. Taylor School of Design in New York City. In 1917, she applied for admission and was accepted. Her design abilities were far more superior to her classmates, and her creations were used as models of exceptional work for the other students. Through those connections as a student, she met affluent clients who appreciated her one-of-a-kind unique designs and the fine quality of her craftsmanship.

In 1946, when actress, Olivia de Havilland accepted the Academy Award for "Best Actress," for her role in the motion picture "To Each His Own," she wore a hand-painted floral Ann Lowe original design. The 1950's marked a significant turning point in Lowe's life and career with the opening of her own store on Madison Avenue, in New York City. As a leading society dressmaker, her designs regularly appeared in the pages of Vogue, Vanity Fair, and Town & Country magazines. She created thousands of gowns, and her evening and bridal wear were sold nationwide at several upscale department stores.

Lowe's name remained well known, mostly to wealthy insiders including the Rockefeller's, DuPont's, and the Roosevelts. Along with numerous department store executives admiring her work, she was well-respected by her clients along with other world renowned designers including, Christian Dior and Edith Head. Her most historically significant commission was the bridal gown and bridal party dresses for the 1953 wedding of Jacqueline Bouvier and then-Senator John F. Kennedy, who would become President of the United States in 1961.

Lowe explained that the driving force behind her work was not a quest for fame or fortune, but a desire to prove that African-Americans can become major players in the world of fashion design. The satisfaction of seeing society women in her dresses often proved to be more than enough. Throughout her pioneering career in fashion design, she lived modestly, commuting from her apartment in Harlem to her office in the Upper East Side of Manhattan.

William Henry Hastie

William Henry Hastie (1904 - 1976) was a leading political pioneer in the 20th century, he was a champion for civil rights during a period when segregation and racial discrimination often went unchallenged. Hastie was a true trailblazer, he was the first African-American appointed as a Federal District Court Judge in the United States. He was appointed to the federal bench in the Virgin Islands by President Franklin D. Roosevelt. Hastie was also one of the first African-American members of Roosevelt's Administration. He was later given the post of Assistant Solicitor for the Department of Interior. While working for the department, he wrote the Constitution for the Virgin Islands, an American territory. He was also the first African-American Governor of a U.S. state or territory to serve a full term. During the 1940's, he was the highest-ranking African-American Judge in U.S. history, surpassed only by Thurgood Marshall in 1976 with his nomination to the Supreme Court. Hastie later received an appointment from President Harry S. Truman for the United States Court of Appeals.

Judge, educator, public official, and civil rights advocate, William Henry Hastie broke through many barriers while fighting for the rights of African-Americans, he used the prominence of his legal position to help make significant changes in the legal system. Growing up in Knoxville, TN., his family relocated to Washington D.C. in 1916, he attended Paul Lawrence Dunbar High School and graduated as valedictorian in 1921. After school he became a teacher in Bordertown N.J, he then attended Harvard Law School, earning his Bachelor's of Law and Doctor of Juridical Science Degree in 1933, he was also a member of Harvard Law review.

Hastie later established a private law practice in Washington, D.C., while also serving as assistant solicitor for the United States Department of the Interior, advising the agency on racial issues. As a lawyer he won several landmark cases on civil rights including one that was overturned by the Supreme Court in his favor. The success of these cases made Hastie a popular figure in the civil rights movement, it lead to him becoming an adviser on racial matters to President Franklin D. Roosevelt in 1933. As an adviser, he drafted legislation which affected politics in the U.S. Virgin Islands, which allowed residents to vote without facing discrimination.

Following the legislation, Hastie was appointed as a District Judge in the U.S. Virgin Islands by President Roosevelt in 1937, the appointment made him the first African-American federal judge in the United States. He served for two years before resigning and becoming Dean of Howard University Law School in 1939. Hastie also served as a law professor during his tenure as Dean at Howard, one of his students was Thurgood Marshall, who later led the Legal Defense Fund for the NAACP and was appointed as a United States Supreme Court Justice.

Later in his career, he worked closely with Marshall as they were lead co-lawyers in the landmark Supreme Court voting rights case of Smith vs. Allwright, which overturned a Texas state law that authorized the legal disenfranchisement of African-American voters. During his time as Dean, Hastie also served as Civilian Aid to Secretary of War, Henry L. Stimson. He advocated for the equal treatment of African-Americans and urged the racial integration of troops during WWII, his protest prompted the Army and Navy to begin with integrated units.

In 1946, President Harry S. Truman appointed Hastie as Governor of the United States Virgin Islands, making him the first African-American to hold this position, he served as governor from 1946 to 1949. Truman also nominated Hastie for Judge of the Third United States Circuit Court of Appeals in 1949, during that time, he became the highest-ranking African-American judge in U.S. history.

John Henry Merrick

In the late 1800's, insurance was unattainable for most African-Americans living in the United States. In 1898, businessman and community leader, John Henry Merrick (1859 - 1919) took the lead in launching the North Carolina Mutual and Provident Association (renamed the North Carolina Mutual Life Insurance Company in 1919), which became the largest African-American-owned business in the country during the time. While serving as the company's first president, Merrick realized the inadequacies and unfair practices of other insurance companies in the state. The founding of the company filled a huge gap, he employed as well as offered insurance policies equally to hundreds of African-American men and women throughout several communities. In 1920, the company had over $2 million in assets. His firm earned Durham, N.C., a reputation as the "Capital of the Black Middle Class." The success of the company and its subsidiaries, most notably the Mechanics and Farmers Bank (1908), brought him national fame as a representative of the "New South," and as vindication for Booker T. Washington's philosophy of attaining self-employment, landownership, and small business. The company's impact, and those of its founders and associates, lasted for generations. They met practical needs, provided insurance, commercial rental opportunities, and other services, while offering a sense of community and pride both to African-American residents of Durham, along with other communities across the country.

Insurance Agent, entrepreneur and business owner, John Henry Merrick was a community leader, and founder of the North Carolina Mutual Life Insurance Company. Born enslaved in Clinton, NC., Merrick lived with his mother and a younger brother. When President Abraham Lincoln signed the Emancipation Proclamation in 1863, his family was free, and they relocated to Chapel Hill, N.C. He found employment making bricks in a brickyard which provided support for his family. At the age of eighteen, he then moved to Raleigh, N.C., where he began work as a brick mason, he participated on the construction of Shaw University.

In 1880, his friend John Wright asked Merrick to join him in relocating to Durham, N.C., to start a new barbershop business. After six months, Wright sold his shares to Merrick making him sole proprietor, eventually he owned eight barbershops. He began buying property in a section of the city known as the Hayti. He bought and built rental properties and by the end of the decade, he was one of the largest property owners in the Hayti.

In 1883, Merrick joined businessmen John Wright, W.A. Day, J.D. Morgan, and T.J. Jones to purchase the Royal Knights of King David, a fraternal lodge which had a successful insurance business. The Royal Knights of David provided inexpensive insurance policies to lodge members. Along with that experience, Merrick in 1898 took the lead in launching the North Carolina Mutual and Provident Association (renamed the North Carolina Mutual Life Insurance Company in 1919), the firm earned Durham a reputation as the "Capital of the Black Middle Class."

Merrick served as President of North Carolina Mutual, which eventually became the largest African-American-owned insurance company in the United States. His success also helped to establish Mechanics and Farmers Bank as well as Lincoln Hospital. Through their efforts Durham, N.C., became an early 20th century city with the greatest concentration of African-American-owned business firms in the country. Merrick thrived and helped others find success in a time of immense racial violence, segregation, and denial of opportunities.

Concerned with more than the economic vitality of Durham, he also participated in efforts to improve the health of Durham's African-American population. In 1901, he served as the first President of the Board of Trustees for Lincoln Hospital. He also met the city's pharmaceutical needs as he founded the Bull City Drug Store. The accomplishments of Merrick and his mutual enterprise was a tremendous source of pride for African-Americans in the city of Durham, it became the foundation of African-American-owned businesses in the country.

Maria Priscilla Williams

Maria Priscilla Williams (1866 - 1932) was a filmmaker, writer, and activist who in 1923, wrote, produced, and acted in the motion picture, "The Flames of Wrath," which made her the first African-American woman film producer in the United States. As a one-time school teacher, she had a history of activism, independence, and interest in the liberal arts. This interest led her first to newspapers, then to film production, scriptwriting, and acting. As a Kansas City, MO., native, she served as the Editor-in-Chief (1891 - 1894) of a weekly newspaper called the "Kansas City Era." This experience peaked her interest to seek greater independence, she then became the founder, writer, and editor of her own newspaper, "The Women's Voice" (1896 - 1900). Williams also became active in politics in the state of Missouri, in 1916, she wrote a memoir on her political and social views titled, "My Work and Public Sentiment." Proceeds from her book were then donated to criminal reform and crime suppression regarding African-Americans throughout the country. In 1916, she married entrepreneur Jesse L. Williams, who owned a movie theater and several other businesses in Kansas City. The pair co-managed the movie theater, which gave the couple experience in distributing and releasing films for African-American audiences during the time. Williams served both as the company's secretary and treasurer. The couple co-founded Western Film Production Company and Booking Exchange.

Educator, activist, director, filmmaker, author, and producer, Maria Priscilla Williams was a trailblazer in the film industry during the early 1900's. Born and raised in Versailles MO., she grew up in the post civil war era of Missouri. She later moved to Kansas City in her early twenties. She began her career working as a Kansas City school teacher in the 1890's for several years. She later gave up teaching in order to become an activist and political writer. Traveling through Kansas as a social activist and lecturer, she often gave politicized speeches on the "topics of the day" for African-American audiences.

Williams settled permanently in Kansas City and shifted towards using newspapers as her outlet for social change. After deciding to end her travels, she became the editor-in-chief for a local Kansas City newspaper called the "New Era." The knowledge and experience she earned led her to independently own and publish her own newspaper called the "Women's Voice," which covered a wide variety of topics.

During the turn of the century, Williams continued to remain an active member of Kansas City's political arena, she published a memoir in 1916 to document her experiences titled, "My Work and Public Sentiment," she also became a national organizer for "The Good Citizens League." She was a self-sufficient woman who was dedicated to creating a difference in her community, she also spearheaded many progressive grassroots movements for African-Americans.

The same year she published her memoir, she married Jesse L. Williams, an entrepreneur who owned several businesses in Kansas City, including a movie theater, which they later managed together as a couple. Their connection to the distribution and release of films for African-American audiences helped her achieve her goal of making her own film. The couple then created a production company, "Western Film Production" in order to independently distribute the film she wanted to make.

In 1923, Williams wrote, produced, and acted in the motion picture, "The Flames of Wrath," which made her the first African-American woman film producer in the United States. The movie was a crime drama that covered tragedy, family, and empathy. Williams knew how to distribute their film to African-American theaters, and it played mostly in the Southern region of the United States. After Williams, there were other female filmmakers of color who emerged that also had a huge impact on African-American films during the 1920s. Together they pioneered an era of cinema that was largely lost in time, but their immense contributions to the film industry were undeniable and a major step forward for future generations.

Dr. James Durham

Dr. James Durham (1762 - 1802) is recognized as the first African-American Physician in the United States. Although he never received a Medical Degree, he was held in the highest regard by many medical practitioners of his era and by the leading physicians of the period. Born enslaved, he changed hands between several enslavers during the early part of his life, some of whom were physicians. As a child, he was taught how to read and write fluently in English, Spanish and French, he was later introduced to medicine and worked as a medical assistant and apprentice. Durham swiftly gained a variety of health related experiences due to his exposure to several medical practices. Encouraged to go into medicine, he purchased his freedom at the age of twenty in 1783 and began practicing medicine in New Orleans, LA. He earned financial success and had a flourishing practice, this was the first recorded instance in the United States of an African-American who was trained in medicine having patients of other racial backgrounds. He treated thousands of patients with Diphtheria and was instrumental in helping to contain the Yellow Fever epidemic that ravaged New Orleans in the late 18th century. During a trip to Philadelphia, PA., in 1788, Durham met Benjamin Rush, the "Father of American Medicine." Durham's expertise on disease treatment and handling epidemics was greatly valued by Rush, he shared Durham's findings with several medical communities across the country.

Recognized historically as America's first African-American physician and entrepreneur, Dr. James Durham was one of the countries most renown doctors during the 18th century. Born enslaved in Philadelphia, PA, he spent most of his early life being taught the fundamentals of reading and writing. Growing up, Durham learned at an early age how to mix medicines and care for patients on a small scale as an assistant. Although he never received a M.D. Degree, as a teenager, he had a medical apprenticeship that was similar to the medical training that most of the 3,500 American trained physicians experienced.

During the American Revolutionary War, he continued to work in medicine, performing tasks for enslavers who were doctors. In 1783, a twenty year old Durham purchased his freedom and began practicing medicine in New Orleans where he earned financial success and a professional distinction. He paid for his liberation from the earnings he received from the patients he treated.

His ability to read and write, as well as his fluency in three languages, English, French, and Spanish, served him well as a community doctor. He was now able to practice medicine independently, specializing in throat medicine. By 1788, Durham established many prominent connections due to his reputation as a reputable physician, he was particularly noted for his treatment of diphtheria cases, a serious infection within the throat and nose.

Durham was instrumental in saving thousands of patients lives during an epidemic of yellow fever that swept through the city of New Orleans, he became the first African-American physician in the country to treat patients of various racial backgrounds. He had a good knowledge of the diseases in his area. He was a respected physician and became infamous for his treatment of diphtheria patients. Durham's success and notoriety caught the attention of Dr. Benjamin Rush, one of the signers of the Declaration of Independence, and one of the most prominent physicians in the United States during the time.

Rush was so impressed with Durham's success in treating diphtheria patients, he tried to convince him to return to Philadelphia and continue his practice there, but Durham chose to remain in New Orleans where he continued to see his patients. The pair formed a professional relationship and maintained a correspondence between 1789 and 1802. Through their letters, Durham and Rush shared their knowledge on disease treatment and handling epidemics. Rush often read Durham's papers on the subject before the College of Physicians of Philadelphia and shared his findings with other prominent members of the medical community.

Fannie Jackson Coppin

Pioneering educator and missionary, Fanny Jackson Coppin (1837 - 1913) is the first African-American School Principal in the United States, she was also the second African-American woman in the country to earn a Bachelor's Degree. For more than 37 years, Coppin was a teacher, then principal of the Institute for Colored Youth (now Cheyney University of Pennsylvania). As an educator and administrator in the mid-1860's, she was not only committed to education, but she also had a passion about helping her students find employment. During her tenure, she made many improvements at the school, she believed that training and education was a pathway towards stable employment and vital to African-Americans becoming self-supporting. She expanded the curriculum to include a vocational training path, which students could choose from ten different trades. Along with being an educator, Coppin was a missionary and a life long advocate for higher education for women. She worked with the African Methodist Episcopal (AME) Church, serving as President of the Women's Home and Foreign Missionary Society. After marrying African Methodist Episcopal Minister, Reverend Levi Jenkins Coppin in 1881, she became interested in missionary work. By 1902, the couple traveled to South Africa to serve as missionaries. While there, the couple established the Bethel Institute, a missionary school featuring self-help programs for South Africans.

Teacher, principal, lecturer, missionary, and champion for education, Fanny Jackson Coppin is the first African-American woman School Principal in the United States. Born enslaved in Washington, D.C., her aunt purchased her freedom in the late 1830's. While spending her childhood years living with her aunt, she eventually relocated to Newport, RI., and spent her teens in the area working as a domestic servant while attending the Rhode Island State Normal School. While there, Coppin gained an appreciation and admiration for the profession of teaching.

Her experience at the school inspired her to pursue higher education for herself, her goal was to become an educator in order to help other African-Americans acquire a formal education. In 1860, she enrolled at Oberlin College, the first college in the United States open to African-American students. Following her graduation in 1865, Coppin relocated to Philadelphia, PA. She accepted a teaching position at the Institute for Colored Youth (now Cheyney University, the oldest HBCU in the United States). The school was established by Quakers with the intent for African-Americans to receive a higher education.

After four years of teaching, Coppin was promoted school principal in 1869, this appointment made her the first African-American principal in the country. During her tenure, she committed herself and the school to ensuring that students were better prepared for real-world work environments. She helped to improve the educational standards for African-Americans in Philadelphia by expanding the school's curriculum with an Industrial Department as well as a Women's Industrial Exchange, she was also committed to community outreach.

Inspired by abolitionist, Frederick Douglass, Coppin often expressed her desire and commitment to educating African-American men and women to become renown intellectuals. As a result of her years of service as a principal, she received an additional appointment as the superintendent, becoming the first African-American in the country to hold such a position. As she continued her career in education, in 1881, she married Reverend Levi Coppin, a notable minister in the African Methodist Episcopal (AME) Church community. The couple worked on a variety of programs as missionaries in South Africa.

Throughout her career, Coppin spent four decades educating others, she conquered overwhelming obstacles and became a beacon for education. In her honor the "Fanny Jackson Coppin Normal School" was established in Baltimore, MD., as a teacher training school. Today, the school is known as Historically Black College and University (HBCU) Coppin State University.

Sources

African-American Inventions That Changed The World: Today in African-American History: African-American Musicians That Changed Music Forever: How Did Black History Month Begin? Michael A. Carson. African-American Museum of History and Culture, Washington, D.C. National Association for the Advancement of Colored People (NAACP), National Inventors Hall of Fame, Douglass, Frederick. My Bondage and My Freedom: The Life and Times of Frederick Douglass. The Autobiography of W. E. B. DuBois. Ebony Magazine, Howard University Library, Collection of Negro Life and History, Black Self-Determination: A Cultural History of the Faith. Beating against the Barriers: Biographical Essays in Nineteenth-Century Afro-American History. Jet Magazine Carter G. Woodson: A Life in Black History. The Roots of African- American Popular History. Doers of the Word: African-American Women Speakers and Writers. How a Radical Social Movement Became an Academic Discipline. Critical Reflections on Black History. The Roots of African American Identity. Mathematicians of the African Diaspora. Library of Congress. Underground Railroad in New York. Encyclopedia Britannica: Guide to Black History. African-American Almanac. Black Women in America. African American National Biography. Black Americans In Congress. The African-American Atlas Black History & Culture an Illustrated Reference. Academy of Motion Picture Arts and Sciences. The World Book Encyclopedia.

ACKNOWLEDGMENTS

As always, I have to begin by giving thanks to God, for guiding my life and giving my family and I his infinite blessings.

To my lovely wife Shenika and our son Matthew.

To my parents, Mary and Sam, who gave me life and taught me how to love God and Family.

To my sister and brother-in-law, Sandra and Arthur.
To my brother and sister-in-law, Sanford and Brigette.
Thank you for your love and support.

To my nieces and nephews, Serena, Stephanie, Shayla, Jayda, Keiana, Darin, Darius and Austin.

To the entire Carson, Street, Hall and Bolden families.
Much love to all of you.

ABOUT THE AUTHORS

Michael and Matthew Carson are a Best-Selling, Award-Winning Father and Son writing team. They are most well known for their publications: "African-American Inventions That Changed The World," "Today In African-American History," "African-American Musicians That Changed Music Forever," and "How Did Black History Month Begin?

Growing up in Queens, New York, Michael has a Bachelor's Degree in Psychology from Virginia State University and works as a Government Analyst. Matthew is a student who enjoys researching and writing about history. Their family currently resides in Atlanta, Georgia.

What began as a conversation with Michael teaching his son Matthew about African-American history, continued into a five book non-fiction series. Together their passion for learning about historical figures grew into a collaboration, and they wanted to educate future generations about the many significant contributions African-Americans have made in our society and the world.

Michael and his wife Shenika co-founded Double Infinity Publishing. Their goal is to publish high quality literature that represents historical facts as well as provide a voice and platform for educating readers.

Made in the USA
Columbia, SC
01 June 2024

36465554R00076